WHOSE LIFE IS IT ANYWAY?

Recognising and Surviving Domestic Violence

Published by Brolga Publishing Pty Ltd
ABN 46 063 962 443
PO Box 12544
A'Beckett St
Melbourne, VIC, 8006
Australia

email: markzocchi@brolgapublishing.com.au

National Library of Australia
Cataloguing-in-Publication data
          Deborah Thomson, author.
          ISBN 9780648150862 (paperback)

A catalogue record for this book is available from the National Library of Australia

Printed in Australia
Cover art by Kelly Lawrence
Cover design by Alice Cannet
Typesetting by Elly Cridland

BE PUBLISHED

Publish through a successful publisher. National Distribution, Dennis Jones & Associates
International Distribution to the United Kingdom, North America.
Sales Representation to South East Asia
Email: markzocchi@brolgapublishing.com.au

WHOSE LIFE IS IT ANYWAY?

Recognising and Surviving Domestic Violence

Deborah Thomson

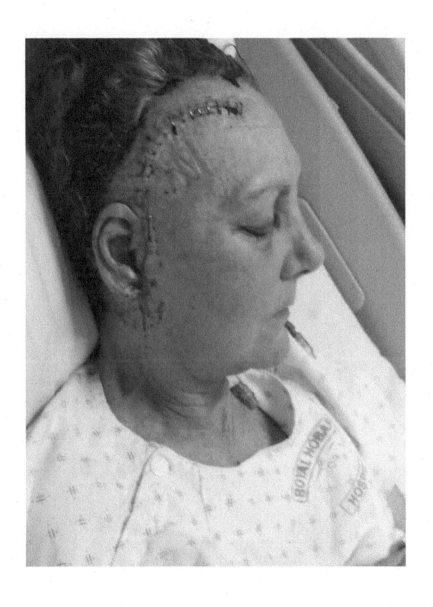

Dedicated to my youngest daughter for encouraging me to leave before it was too late.

Acknowledgements

I wish to acknowledge my mother, Laurie Gilbert, without whom I would not be here today writing my account. I may have had the courage to leave the abuse in theory; however, without Laurie I would not have known how to put that into practice. Her patience over the years following my exit from the marital home has been inspirational.

I also wish to acknowledge my wonderful partner P. B, who not only inspired me to write this book but also patiently edited it, ironing out the occasional ramblings within its pages. His love and guidance has lifted me to greater heights than I would have thought possible.

I thank my good friends Debra Button and Ros Muir who have gotten behind my campaign in ways other than donating alone to promote this book's publication. Their support has helped make my words a printed reality.

Lastly, I wish to acknowledge my three daughters, in particular my youngest, whose bravery and compassion knows no bounds.

Preface

Abuse of a person may be threefold. First, there is the direct abuse by the perpetrator. Abuse can also take the form of a complete lack of remorse by the abuser and their refusal to apologise for their actions or recognise their fault at all. Thirdly, abuse may occur when friends, family or the general public, after finding out about the domestic violence, aim condemnation and judgment at the sufferer for either staying with the abuser or leaving and then returning to the perpetrator. Thus, abuse may be indirectly perpetrated when people around the victim are aware of the violence but choose to ignore it, often arguing that it's a domestic issue or none of their business. Overall, the judgment of others, the stigma associated with being a victim of domestic violence and the accompanying feeling of being a pariah in society compound the self-hatred and low self-esteem of the victim. Rather than judgment, compassion and support from others is most necessary.

Throughout the relationship, I felt utter contempt for myself partly because I accepted his abuse but also because his violence did not compel me to leave when it should have. Wayne took my personal contempt and ran with it, using it for his own abusive purposes. In my mind, I had legitimate reasons to stay, irrespective of the abuse I'd received. This should have alerted me to just how dangerous my capacity for self-deception was. I was emotionally, sexually and physically assaulted on numerous occasions yet continued to justify Wayne's behaviour to myself. Because self-deception is often a primary causal factor in an abused person's decision to stay, it is imperative that outside professional help is sought as quickly as possible into an abusive relationship to clarify what is *really happening* between persecutor and victim. I hope that readers who may currently find themselves in situations similar to mine will recognise the importance of keeping a clear mind and the ability to see the abuse as others see it: reprehensible and extremely difficult to fix in isolation.

There are reasons shared by the majority of abusers as to why they abuse others. An abuser may have had continued exposure to others in the family being abused. Repeated exposure will result in abusive behaviour becoming 'normalised' and the child sees these behaviours as an inevitable part of the family dynamics, the way arguments are resolved between family members. Abusing family members becomes a learned behaviour in adulthood. Perhaps they themselves were abused in childhood and to resolve this abuse they use matching abusive measures in adulthood.

An abuser may have an untreated disorder such as anti-social personality disorder or a psychopathy where they derive pleasure from witnessing others' pain especially when they are the ones inflicting the pain.

There may be unresolved anger issues that result in anger

becoming uncontrolled and unmanaged. Poor impulse control, unresolved trauma or drug and alcohol abuse together with excessive pent-up anger invariably lead to a 'short fuse' whereby the smallest or totally unrelated event triggers an outward explosive display of anger that seemingly comes from nowhere.

Abusers often lack empathy, are narcissistic or lack an accurate perception of reality; they can't see their own behaviour as abusive so they keep doing it.

In the majority of cases, abusers have control issues; they have to be in charge and remain in control by using domination and intimidation (www.pro.psychocentral.com|2017). Acknowledging why certain people abuse others does not justify behaviours. However, understanding the abuse and recognising it for what it really is will help the abused take positive steps to remove themselves from abusive situations.

There are crucial warning signs that domestic violence (defined by professional social workers as the systematic, wilful pattern of power and control perpetrated by one intimate partner against another) is occurring within the relationship.

Crucial signs indicative of abuse include:

EXCLUSIVE COMMITMENT – There is a strong pressure from the other for exclusive commitment in the relationship. The abuser comes on strong, quickly, and often threatens to leave if you don't move in with them.

JEALOUSY - The abuser is constantly jealous. Prior to living with you, they call or visit often, usually without notice.

CONTROLLING BEHAVIOURS – These behaviours can take

the form of interrogations such as constantly asking where you've been or who you've seen that day. You are required to get permission to go somewhere or do something. This often happens very early in a relationship.

PSYCHOLOGICAL ABUSE – This is a form of manipulation which leads to the victim losing their sense of reality and ability to discern unacceptable from acceptable behaviours. Very quickly this ability is diminished to the point where you accept abusive behaviour as something normal.

UNREALISTIC EXPECTATIONS – Abusers want perfection from you and expect you to meet their every need (even though it is often impossible to know what they expect or what their needs are as both continually change, often rapidly). You are expected to live your life for the sole purpose of fulfilling their needs, to obey, serve and wait on the abuser. Hypercriticism is a frequent component of this trait which leads to constant put-downs exemplified by phrases such as: 'I love you, but …'

ISOLATION – You find yourself increasingly isolated from your friends and family. As this happens, the abuser also refuses to communicate with you unless on their own terms. They ignore or exclude you or they constantly speak to you using sarcasm or belittling tones.

REFUSAL TO ADMIT RESPONSIBILITY – Others are always to blame. The abuser never believes they are at fault. This is another form of mental abuse where the abuser convinces you that you are solely to blame for the abuse and that it is your responsibility alone to change. You are made responsible for their feelings: you must make them feel better, you make them angry. Comments such as: 'I wouldn't act this way if you didn't ...' and similar ones are recurrent.

EMOTIONAL CONTROL - Guilt-trips are commonly used to control you. Abusers dictate the way you feel and withdraw their affection if you don't act the way they want you to.

HYPERSENSITIVITY / VICTIMISATION - Abusers are hypersensitive, ranting and raving about the injustices they experience that are actually just a part of living.

MOOD SWINGS - They have sudden mood swings, from anger to calm and vice versa in a matter of minutes. When calm, the abuser will usually deny that an abusive incident occurred or they will diminish its import.

CRUELTY - They can be cruel to animals and/or children or those weaker than them.

ABUSIVE SEXUAL BEHAVIOURS - When sex is forceful the abuser says it is 'play'. You are forced to engage in unwanted sex.

HISTORY OF VIOLENCE - There is a past history of battery. They may admit it but will insist that the other person brought it on themselves.

THREATS - Abusers often use threats of violence to obtain what they want from you. They might say: 'I'll shoot you if you don't ...' then dismiss the threat or argue they didn't mean it. Another commonly used threat is: 'If you don't ..., I will ...'

These crucial signs of abuse in the home were frequent in my relationship with Wayne. The first nine of the signs above dominated our relationship between 1985 and 1989 with intermittent physical violence defining the relationship. The latter years, as Wayne gained greater control and therefore an increased sense of security, became dominated by physical and sexual violence although the emotional and psychological abuse continued.

The warning signs above are shown throughout the book by the symbol # and linked to events which, by their nature, exemplify an abuser's behaviour. This system will hopefully clarify the ways in which crucial warning signs are manifest in an abusive relationship. Perhaps by seeing specific examples, a victim of abuse will really understand just how precarious their safety is while they remain in the relationship. I also hope seeing those signs will make it harder for the victim to persist in the belief, even in their own mind, that they are not being abused, or that an abuser's behaviour can be attributed to bad moods only. I have placed the symbol alongside only one or two examples that highlight each warning sign, rather than every example, to encourage free-flowing reading and to avoid cluttering the story itself.

As I write this, I am recovering from neurosurgery involving the clipping of two aneurysms (see photo above) that are highly likely to be the result of past head injuries from domestic violence incidents. The head wounds I got during the incidents—the first where my head was slammed into a brick wall thrice, the second where I was tackled, with my forehead hitting the bitumen road—coincided with the areas in my brain where the aneurysms sit, so one can reasonably conclude that domestic violence caused the aneurysms to develop. The surgeons are in agreement, concurring that aneurysms are most likely to result either from head injury or a genetic predisposition, which I do not have. Recovery is slow and painstaking. I was extremely ill during the first fortnight in hospital, hardly able to lift my head from the pillow and for many days managing to eat only three spoonsful of soup.

It has now been a further two weeks since returning home and I have to be assisted with everything as my right eyelid is still closed from the trauma of the operation. The inability to see properly is impacting on my mobility and my mental state. My dependence on others to care for me and the snail-like progress of my recovery compels me to implore persons in abusive relationships to leave early before something similar happens to them. If I had been made aware of the warning signs pointing to an abuser's profile early in my relationship, I would have been far more likely to leave before sustaining the head injuries that caused this current nightmare.

Introduction

Names of people and places have been changed. With the exception of the Gold Coast and Sydney, all names are fictional to protect the innocent and not so innocent.

My partner drops a knife on the wooden floor just behind me. The loud noise causes me to jump high in my seat. It makes me wonder whether I'll ever be entirely free of my reactions after the experience I have had with domestic violence prior to meeting Phillip.

Now, I am dogged by post-traumatic stress and the endless analysis of the choices that led me to stay with an extremely violent man for seventeen years. Then, I was being swept along by the need to survive; the hyper vigilance strangely coupled with an attitude of extreme indifference to the horror story unfolding. As a measure of my insanity (I can only think that I must have had a degree of insanity to stay with a man who, from the onset, was violent toward me) and regardless of the high level of abuse, I subjugated my true self in order to fit with Wayne's idea of what being a real woman meant. Who I was quickly became superfluous. Staying alive and figuring out the key to stopping Wayne's violence mattered more. It may seem odd to readers that at the onset of his abuse I could still leave relatively easily, but chose to remain. That I stayed will be incomprehensible to many. It was by virtue of Wayne's skills of indoctrination that he gained complete control of my thoughts and actions. His conditioning resulted in my total acquiescence. Ultimately, having three daughters to this man, the financial security our marriage and business afforded me and the constant mental manipulation and physical intimidation on his part all stymied my leaving. It was easier to stay in isolation than to face the unknown outside the home. Such was my life when my grip on reality disappeared.

This book is an attempt to explain what is perhaps unexplainable: why the abuse to which I was subjected occurred. I also hope to shed some light on the reasons why I stayed, left and then returned, even after the violence, and particularly in the beginning when it should have been so much easier to leave. Yet, perhaps it can't be explained to—or understood by—anyone other than those who've experienced mistreatment at the hands of their partner. I expect that most people, outside of abusive relationships, will wonder why a person who is being abused stays in such a relationship and when or if they leave, why they sometimes return. These are questions I have also asked myself a multitude of times. I can only say that Wayne exerted a form of brainwashing on me which caused me to believe that staying was the best and only option available to me at the time. Coupled with that belief were my natural introversion, naivety, social anxiety and shyness around others, all of which left me vulnerable to an unscrupulous man with mental problems of his own. While

I chose to remain, he also chose to continue abusing me, and regardless of whether I stayed or left, nothing mitigates or excuses his reprehensible behaviour.

I have written this book using my actual diary entries to document exactly what occurred as it happened rather than relate my story wholly as a narrative. I hope this format will help make my experiences as real as possible while providing the reader with a clearer picture of what constituted daily life for me and for, I am sure, many others, both now and then. Note that these entries, in particular the early ones, are written with some degree of immaturity, despite my being twenty-four in 1985. Yet, they are indicative of my mental and social development at the time which I regard as slightly backward compared to my peers inasmuch as my innocence and naivety made me less capable of detecting people with dubious intentions.

At the time of the first diary entries, I was sharing a unit with my friend Narene with whom I attended university in Alka Springs. We were in the third and last year of our Bachelor degrees and both of us intended to pursue post-graduate studies the following year. At the time I met Wayne, I was seeing a kind man called Michael. With plummeting self-esteem and little self-confidence, I was hitting a low point which prevented me from seeing Michael's worth. My state of mind left me open to Wayne's 'charms'. When we first met, he acted as though I was the most interesting and attractive female he'd talked to in a long time. This was balm to my bruised sense of self. His attentiveness made him stand out from others and despite misgivings I allowed him into my life. He became integral to alleviating my loneliness and the feeling I had of being a misfit in society. His constant talking dispelled fears that I was boring and unable to carry a conversation. I didn't have to contribute too much while he held the floor, and this suited me just fine.

As our relationship progressed, Wayne withdrew his conversation while similarly isolating me from others, resulting in more time spent alone with him. Sustained togetherness did not result in our getting to know each other. Rather, Wayne used this time to belittle me relentlessly or he'd refuse to converse with me for days. This was so different to his initial 'romancing' and the constant attention he had given me that it exacerbated my confusion and lack of belief in my ability to attract and hold someone's interest.

I can't explain why I allowed his abuse to continue when I had never been the subject of anything similar in the past. I had never been a 'doormat' before but, somehow, I slipped into that role almost as soon as the relationship began. Wayne's behaviour was, even then, unacceptable. I railed against it whenever it occurred yet couldn't drag myself out of the strange inertia I felt when he abused me. I was simultaneously angry with him and detached from his behaviour. It was as if I were split in two. I wanted to leave the first time his violence expressed itself yet another part of me blamed myself for his actions. I became incredibly determined to fix him and create the relationship I imagined we could have. After some years of marriage, I knew that my imagined relationship would never materialise. It then became a matter of surviving each day with mind, body and soul intact.

1985

Friday 21st June

Narene and I went to the Republic Hotel. Wayne, Ian, (friend of Wayne's) *Narene and I were by the bar. I went and sat at a table and Wayne came over and raved to me. He said he'd wanted to 'crack onto me'* (this phrase was part of the vernacular of the young in 1985) *at the Mentals concert. When he said that, I vaguely remembered on that night a thin dark looking guy standing at the fringes of our group, staring at me. Narene, Wayne and I danced then he was supposed to come over our place but Michael* (on again off again boyfriend), *Narene and I went to Impies* (Imperial Hotel) *and I didn't see Wayne again that night.*

Friday 16th August

Narene and I went to the Flye Inn then as we were walking to Impies we ran into Julian (friend of Wayne's) *and Wayne and they followed us to Impies. Wayne sat beside me at the bar and raved on again about how he wanted to go out with me, that he was attracted to me and didn't know why and he asked what my 'scene with Michael was'. He then said he'd wait until 'I sorted my head out' and then pursue me.*

Wednesday 28th August

I went to bed at midnight and Wayne turned up but I only talked to him through my bedroom window. He later said he knew from that moment on that I didn't want him otherwise I would have just invited him into my bedroom then. He said he wouldn't try again.

I remember while writing this entry originally that on that night I was annoyed by Wayne's presence at the unit every day and the fact that he was never giving notice prior to visiting. # I was also annoyed that Wayne had assumed that he could come to my bedroom window whenever he pleased and I would welcome him in as though his was normal behaviour. Not inviting him in that night shows that my instinct about Wayne (his persona had lately felt a little 'off') was working properly at the time. However, the more he pursued me with his declarations of love and adoration, the more my ability to be objective and see through him, disappeared. I can't believe that I fell for his 'romancing' which was essentially a form of stalking. Knowing that I let him into my life makes me feel disgusted and angry with myself for being so gullible and accepting of behaviours that initially had aggravated me.

Tuesday 10th September

Narene and I went up to the uni (University of Alka Springs) bistro on her moped. Wayne was there and came over and said that he only came over our place now because Bob (a friend of Wayne's) wanted him to. He told me that he couldn't come over as a friend anymore because he couldn't accept being with me when he knew that I didn't want to take things further. He then got really angry and uptight and left. # 'So, we can't even be friends,' I thought.

His wanting and expecting exclusive commitment from me so soon after he'd met me is a crucial warning sign. It was all or nothing with him. He did not have the patience to watch our friendship perhaps develop romantically and was often frustrated and annoyed that I was not moving emotionally at the same pace that he was. Or should I say I was not tolerating nor accepting of his control as rapidly as he would have liked me to.

Monday 14th October

Narene told me Bob is trying to match-make Wayne with me as he's rapt in me. Wayne had told him at the Flye Inn that he was in love with me.

When I heard this, I thought that maybe I could give Wayne a chance. I was doomed not to have anyone else (this was my pathetic thinking at that time). Michael must have had a new girlfriend as I never saw him out at night and Bill (another man who had previously expressed a desire to further our friendship) was neatly tucked away with his new girlfriend. And now Narene, my best friend, had Bob. I felt so strongly that I was alone and left out and that feeling made me a little desperate.

Tuesday 15th October

Wayne turned up tonight and we watched a movie but he kept trying to talk over the dialogue saying 'This is boring. I came over to talk not sit staring at the TV.' He left at 10, halfway through the movie. Later in bed I had a horrible dream about black magic and Wayne brutally murdering these people and also trying to kill Nareen and myself in our flat. I woke feeling depressed from the dream and remained depressed the following day. I remember feeling low because of the sense I got from the dream that Wayne could be capable of violence even though he had not openly exhibited such tendencies. Despite that feeling I still examined what of my behaviours caused him to leave suddenly last night. This too, contributed to my dejection.

This was one of many episodes of depression at the time that left me vulnerable to being preyed upon by Wayne, a control addict dressed in amenable, sociable and attentive clothes.

Wednesday 23rd October

Wayne has been coming over every day, of course without prior notice. # When I casually mentioned that it might be helpful if he could let me know that he'd be visiting he brushed my comment aside, saying that he was being spontaneous and so enamoured that he just had to see me and didn't have time to ask for my permission to see me. Tonight, he said I was so crazy and different he couldn't work me out. We are getting along really well and he's very affectionate. It's great for a change having a male that's rapt in me.

Later counselling showed me that his overly attentive behaviour, while flattering at the time, was really a systematic grooming of me to ensure my absolute loyalty. #

Friday 25th October

Wayne and I were now boyfriend and girlfriend. He came over early and woke me and I cooked him breakfast.
Tonight he, Narene, Ian and I walked to Jenny's (a friend of Wayne's) where a party was happening. Everyone kept coming

over to Wayne and I on the lounge shaking Wayne's hand and saying: 'You have a new woman, good for you.' Al (friend of Wayne's) *got us Bourbons but after the first one I felt sick. I went outside as I felt uncomfortable with Michael* (my old boyfriend who was also at the party) *on the other side of the lounge room staring at me. Two guys came outside and sat down beside me chatting and Wayne came out just then. He said: 'Are you ready to leave?' in a filthy voice and gave us all filthy looks to go with the voice. He was well and truly angry with me. He's so jealous. #*
We walked home and had sex despite how sick I was. #

Never in our relationship did I use sex to manipulate Wayne. Rather he used it as a weapon to manipulate me. Later I noticed a pattern where Wayne would demand sex whenever he was jealous of other men or when he was feeling unsure of my affection because I'd done something that didn't suit him. His sexual domination together with my acquiescence to his demands increased his sense of security.

Saturday 26th October

Wayne said he hoped we'd stay together as he really liked and trusted me. I think I'm starting to like him but I'm sure I'm boring him as he seems to get down and rather quiet when he's around me. I still find it hard to talk to him; he's not open to me and hardly listens to me. #

I didn't realise it at the time but Wayne had unrealistic expectations of our relationship and very different ideas to me regarding what I should have said and done to make him feel better (another crucial warning sign). He expected perfection from me wherein I was supposed to provide scintillating conversation even though he often told me how boring I was or that I was such a 'ball and chain' that he was justified in not making conversation with me at all. He expected and demanded that I wait on him, obey him, in short, meet his every need. These needs extended to feeding his voracious appetite for sex and to dress provocatively both at home and in public. The bugbear with the latter was that I would dress to go out in high heels, stockings and short, tight dresses as per his instructions, feel utterly uncomfortable in this style of dress and as the night progressed, increasingly distraught because Wayne would become belligerent and abusive due to the stares and attention I'd receive from other males. Wayne would inevitably accuse me of encouraging other men when it was him who had forced me to wear such clothes in the first place! Alternatively, he would often accuse me of being slovenly and that I should 'dress up' more to enhance my looks. He constantly told me that I was 'ugly' when dressed in house clothes, the inference being that if I made the effort to dress to his liking I would be much more appealing and worth his time and effort. Wayne seemed to think that if he continued to be hypercritical of my appearance (he constantly compared me to other girls he knew or to television personalities where I would fall far short of their looks and style) this would compel me to always look my best in his presence.

Saturday 2nd November

Went to a disco at the Grand (hotel) *and I was happy. Wayne turned up and was distant and we hardly talked. He said: 'I saw you in a car earlier with Dave and Carl,'* (both friends of Wayne's)

*and he became annoyed and ignored me then. As we were leaving
the Grand the aforementioned Dave gave me a hug and kiss and
Wayne accused me of 'pashing him off'.* In his caravan (Wayne
lived in his parent's van in their backyard as he couldn't afford
a rental while he was in a low paying job at the time) *he said
he was so angry about me being in Dave's car and not letting
him know. # All I had done was get a lift downtown with the
man. He became really agitated and in a dirty mood and said:
'I don't know where your morals are. All women are the same.'
He then screamed: 'I hate you all and I'm always getting hurt
by you bitches.' # Every time I'd say something to defend myself
or to try to calm him he'd yell at me that he didn't trust me and
couldn't handle being hurt again. He wouldn't listen to me when
I said the kiss was nothing to worry about and he yelled that he
wouldn't forget it and he should go and flirt with a chick in front
of me and see how I liked it. We got around to having sex after
that, at his insistence, but I was so uptight from his yelling at me
that I couldn't 'perform' well. Sleep eluded me also so I tried to get
Wayne to talk about it but he wouldn't, he just kept saying: 'You
forget about it. I know I won't.' I despair when guys are angry and
won't talk about their feelings or build mountains of meaning from
insignificant events. # Wayne's behaviour is so typical of that, he is
full of pride and paranoia about women. He was shouting so loud
his parents would have heard it all but when I mentioned that to
him later (about his yelling being heard) he brushed it off and said
they scream at each other all the time so it'd make no difference
to them. I went to sleep at 3am. This incident was one of many
interrogations I'd endured by Wayne regarding who I'd talked to
that day, where I'd been and what I'd done with whom. He often*

implied that I needed his permission for whatever I'd planned to do on the day and that I was somehow being underhanded if I did not seek this permission. # He would also see any innocent gesture of affection that I'd give to other males as indicative of my loose morals or as evidence of an imminent break-up with him. Even though yet another meaningless event (my lift with Dave) had been blown out of all proportion, given his assumptions of my lowly character, he was in his mind justified in verbally and sexually abusing me.

Thursday 12th December

Wayne rang again tonight before we went out (I'd gone to the Gold Coast to see family for Christmas and had only been there for four days) *and asked me if I'd gotten the letter from him saying how much he missed me and how he was depressed and couldn't stop thinking about when we'd be back together and out raging. Then he got angry for my not calling him first # and said I sounded like I had a cold. Last time he rang he'd asked me if I was drunk. Said he hated talking to me on the phone and wasn't used to it. Then he said: 'I'm coming up in the van Friday night and I'll be there Saturday morning,' because he didn't like me 'hanging around all those millionaires'.*

Despite 'hiccups' we were still together at the closing of 1985. In my mind, I was lucky to be with anyone at all. I knew he had problems, but they seemed to be minor ones which might be ironed out the longer we were together. I was seeing the relationship in the context of Wayne being 'normal' while he saw me in a completely different way as someone who would put up with his abusive behaviour and therefore, useful to him. As I write this I begin to understand that already my sense of reality was skewed to his advantage. His abuse though not violent yet, was insidiously soul-destroying. Worse than that I justified Wayne's behaviour and felt that the longer we were together the more I would convince him of my ability to improve his life, and in so doing, prove my usefulness to him.

1986

Thursday 6th February

Talked to Wayne's mother in her kitchen then went out to the van and we seemed to be getting on when suddenly Wayne said he wanted to break it off because it was too much of a 'spin out' seeing me all the time; he needed to be alone a lot and felt that he had to come out and see me even when he wanted to be alone. Said I was perfect and the best girl a guy could hope for BUT ... he didn't know if he was doing the right thing but he'd handled it (having to see me constantly) until now. He said he couldn't any longer and not to wait for him though he'd waited eight months for me. I felt sick thinking that I'd somehow caused yet another relationship to disintegrate then he laughed (as if breaking up meant nothing) and said: 'What are you doing tomorrow?' Then he said: 'You're not too badly off. It's not another chick, and you're the only one on my mind.' I didn't want to discuss it anymore so left and as I was leaving he went to kiss me but I turned my head away. Went home and sat thinking awful paranoid thoughts about how no one wanted me, how I had no friends in Alka Springs and how Wayne would be out partying and not sitting at home alone. (He did go out that night and nicely informed me he had the best night out in ages.) *He came out late in the night in his mother's car but I didn't answer the door. What a disgusting night of awful, black, desperate thoughts.*

Friday 7th February

Wayne turned up at midnight and said: 'Do you want to go to a party at Liz and Toby's?' (Wayne's friends) *I said no and he yelled from his car: 'You're being bitchy, are you annoyed?' He deigned to stay rather than party 'despite the sacrifice' and said it'd only taken him a day to realise that he wanted to still go out with me. I asked him what his reasons for that really were. He said he just wanted to, then confessed that his mum had kicked him out of her house and wouldn't let him back in when he told her we'd broken up, saying to him: 'You're throwing away a good lady.' I am wary of his motivations and don't know whether we'll get on any better than we did before but I agreed to see how it goes with us back together.*

Here is another indication of my inability to sever ties with Wayne.

Sunday 9th February

Terrible that Wayne needs to be drunk before he can be friendly to me. # Makes me wonder why he still sees me. He's so sarcastic with me like he used to be with Sharon (an ex-girlfriend, not the same 'love of my life' Sharon) *whom he never really liked. He never listens to me like he thinks I'm some sort of adornment and nothing else. # Ken* (an old friend of mine from Urindy) *came over at the Grand to talk to me and Wayne got angry and practically dragged me out of the hotel. # We left and went back to his caravan. He said I had to turn him on so we had sex.*

Then he wanted me to go home immediately after, which upsets me as if he can't bear me around for a minute longer, like some sort of prostitute. It was pouring rain and lightning was flashing in the sky when I left the van yet Wayne didn't care whether I was inconvenienced or nervous. The storm continued while I walked home.

Saturday 15th February

When we got back from the Flye Inn the glass door on the van (Wayne's caravan) was broken where it had been glued and Wayne chucked a tantrum over it then started on me saying that all guys sleep with anything they can find. When I said: 'So it doesn't matter if it is me or not,' he said: 'Sex is sex, the object of it is to get it off.' I then said: 'I thought I meant a bit more than that,' and he replied: 'Do you think you're the best I've ever had?' and laughed. He was a real bastard, saying he had no respect for Narene going out with Bob who was 'screwing behind her back' and that I was no higher in his esteem than her with his friend. He was getting really worked up, more and more rude and sarcastic so when he said: 'What are you waiting for? Turn me on, you're the only girl I know who waits for the guy to ask,' I had sex with him to calm him down. He said if he didn't give it to me enough I'd be off 'screwing someone else' so he did it to keep me from looking elsewhere, and that he didn't feel any more for me than he does anyone else in bed. All women are 'sluts', he said. He has such a thing about this. #

I am loath to say that despite his licentious and provocative litany I continued to convince myself that if I gave him enough love and attention I would somehow change his thinking regarding women and increase his security. Why did I always put aside my doubts and fears about this relationship, divest myself of pride, self-respect and self-worth to instead subjugate and humiliate myself for an unattainably loving partnership?

Saturday 22nd March

Went to Tatts, and Harry (friend of Wayne's) asked Wayne if he liked my looks and he said: 'Of course I do. She's my woman.' He said I was pretty but I wasn't a lady. I dressed like a guy, he said, but that was okay because he was no gentleman. This guy stood close to me and said: 'You'd be good for a fuck,' and Wayne spun around saying: 'What did you say to my lady?' They argued then the guy grabbed Wayne around the ears and they started fighting. Wayne was pushed to the ground and the fight stopped. This altercation put him in an aggressive mood. We left when the pub closed and I smiled at an old guy who apparently had said something rude to me only I didn't hear it and Wayne did. When we got to the bus stop, he started screaming at me saying: 'I've been waiting six months for a smile like the one you gave a filthy old man.' He kept screaming and I couldn't believe what was happening. # He said: 'You're driving me crazy. I'm in love with you and it's not the man's job to keep saying it. You've never said it to me, never,' then he pushed me. I fell on my backside so hard my shoe flew off and Wayne got down on his hands and knees and said: 'I didn't push you, you fell. # You're making an arse of yourself, get up.' I got up and he screamed into my face again. I cried so he grabbed my chin and kept grabbing it yelling at me to 'stop fucking howling'. I got angry and pushed his hand away and said: 'Don't touch me like that.' We went back to his van and had sex because he wanted to. #

Just whose life is it anyway?

This was the beginning of the physical violence, as it occurred I remember being shocked, horrified and sick at heart yet at the same time believing that I'd caused it. Why else would an apparently sane person who professed to love me manhandle me if it were not something I'd done to instigate his abusive behaviour?

Saturday 29th March

Wayne has been constantly harassing about me moving in with him and wanted me to ask Narene to ask Peter (her new boyfriend whom she married three years later) *to move in with her. He kept talking about me getting away from Narene. 'She's no good as she's just using you for half the rent,' he said and told me I'd be better off with him and dumping her as a friend. I'm still very apprehensive at the thought of moving in with Wayne whom I'll never be comfortable with totally, but who else is there in my life? If I say no to his proposition, would he really leave me? Could I risk that?*

It was all or nothing where Wayne was concerned. Whenever he spoke of us moving in together it would be in the form of an ultimatum: if I didn't move in now it would mean the end for us, I had to move or we would split, etc. #

This was the pivotal point in my sorry saga; my next choice would determine the nature of our relationship. Future events would show I made the wrong choice.

Thursday 3rd April

Wayne keeps going on about my dress sense saying I dress like a 'druggie' and should have more pride in myself. He called the white pants I had on today 'rags' and I hate when he carries on like that especially when in another breath, he says: 'Don't worry, dress as you like, I love you anyway.' He always finds ways to lay the blame for his discontent onto me. # It is obvious from what he says to me that I must be the one to change, be a more interesting conversationalist, a better cook, dress up more, acquiesce to everything, his list of demands goes on forever and I madly try to tick each list item off. # He occasionally blames his mother for his hatred of women, or past girlfriends for making him a jealous person but it is mainly me who bears the blame. #

One of his main weapons of abuse when he blamed me for a so-called infraction, would be to withdraw his attention or affection (public affection only for appearance's sake, at home he did not show affection or gestures were perfunctory, leading to sex) if he deemed that I was not trying hard enough to make him feel better. Guilt trips were so common they became almost ineffective as a means to condition my behaviour.

Friday 4th April

Went to his parents for dinner and Wayne told them how I'd been on his back all day, when it was really him who'd been yelling at me. Went home to get ready to go out and Wayne arrived and saw Narene in a dress and me in jeans. He later carried on about how great Narene looked and that I was only in jeans. He told me I should start dressing like her because I was much prettier than her, however guys would choose her over me by the way she dressed.

We argued all the way to Tatts then sat not talking. Later he said he loved me no matter how I dressed but if he was 'a chick, he'd get right into dressing up'. What a day. No matter what I did or said it was like he hated me or thought I was stupid. # He's very selfish and does what he wants. I have to go along with it.

What an incredible statement! Why on earth would anyone think that they had to *go along with any form of abuse?* I cringe in disgust as I rewrite this diary entry.

Sunday 20th April

Wayne arrived at 6.15 for dinner at 6.30. Peter (Narene's boyfriend) *came too. We had pumpkin soup first and straightaway Wayne was angry as he hated pumpkin and didn't eat it. Had a roast for second course. The dinner was a disaster: Wayne was really rude to me all night and Peter sat with his mouth open at the way Wayne was talking to me and nearly threw his dessert at him he was so disgusted. After dinner Wayne and I sat in the lounge room saying nothing while Peter and Narene were in the kitchen laughing and having a ball. Went to bed and Wayne yelled at me saying that I knew he hated that soup but went ahead and gave it to him anyway, embarrassing him in front of everybody. I said that he'd acted like he hated my guts in front of everybody and he said that I was imagining everything. # I was stupid enough to have sex then to calm him down and he said: 'See you in the morning sweetheart,' after being so aggressive the entire evening. #*

Diminishing the import of abusive behaviours upon another or denying that abuse has occurred at all is a crucial warning sign that I was with an abuser. Wayne's sudden mood swing from anger to calmness as a means to achieve his own ends is typical of abusive behaviour as well. That the above incident did not result in physical violence was due to his staying overnight in someone else's home, in the company of friends who would not have tolerated abuse. That his abuse on the night was limited because we weren't alone suggests that a perpetrator's common statement: 'I was out of control when it happened,' may often not be the case since they have sufficient control not to radically abuse when there are witnesses, saving the stronger abuse for home when alone with the victim. Unfortunately, violence often did occur within our own house, often triggered by less than Wayne's feeling embarrassed.

Counselling showed me that domestic abuse is mainly due to what is termed the cycle of violence. This cycle is typical for most perpetrators in that there is a build-up of tension within the abuser which leads to belittling, criticism and blame directed at the abused. The abuser then explodes as the tension reaches a critical point in their psyche and they feel a massive release in the form of screaming (verbal abuse) or physical abuse of the victim. Finally, there is the honeymoon phase as tension dissipates and endorphins flood the brain. At this point the abuser may become 'loving', promising 'it will never happen again' (that is, if they refer to the incident at all). It is vital that readers, particularly those within a new relationship with an abuser, understand that protestations of lack of control on the abuser's part, that the victim is to blame for the abuser's behaviours or that the violence is a one-off and will never be repeated, are purely the vocal result of the euphoria the abuser feels post-release of the stress and tension that has been building over a matter of days. In the majority of cases, the tension will increase again and inevitably be released through new instances of abusive behaviours, hence what is coined the cycle of abuse: the behaviours are learned, habitual, repetitive and cyclic.

Tuesday 22nd April

I didn't see Wayne all day so rang him at 4pm and he yelled at me saying he and his mother had been waiting all day for me to come over (first I knew about this arrangement) *and he was furious, hardly talked, then hung up. His mother later told me that Wayne said to her he was 'through with that lunatic woman forever'. It was too bad if I'd wanted to spend time today with my Mum and Grandma who'd come from the Gold Coast to see me for my birthday.* #

This was the last time I 'defied' Wayne and spent an entire day alone with my family, without him giving me permission to do so. From then on, I had to ask, often beg, to be allowed to spend quality time alone with Mum and Grandma even though they'd make a long trip—which they could hardly afford—from the Gold Coast, just to spend a few days to see me once a year in Alka Springs.

Wednesday 23rd April

Feel so depressed about yesterday. Mum says he's (Wayne) on the defensive because he's so obsessed with me. I rang Wayne later to tell him about a big drug bust Grandma and I had witnessed on the uni grounds and he interrupted saying: 'I don't want to hear about that. I want to see you, is that all you have to say?' then he said: 'I'm too upset over yesterday. I'll talk to you in the next few days,' so I hung up on him while he was still ranting.

Saturday 3rd May

I went into town and bought a pink jumper to match my shoes and bag. Not looking forward to tonight at all and felt worse when Wayne picked me up to go and said nothing about my looks. We sat at the bar at Rotary House where the 21st (Kathy, an exgirlfriend of Wayne's) *birthday party was and Danny* (friend of Wayne's) *and Chrissie* (who Wayne had once gone out with), *stood with Wayne and I. We got a table for four. I accidentally spilt a beer all over the table and of course Wayne got angry about it even though he himself spilt one a few minutes later. Wayne and I hardly talked, and when he did, it was to say that Kathy* (the girl whose 21st we attended) *'had class and she was a top lady' because she could keep up with Wayne's drinking. 'Once she even drank me under the table and I was really proud of her,' he said. When Kathy came over to the table to talk to us, he couldn't keep his eyes off her and continued staring at her after she'd left, ignoring me the rest of the night. # I said I was leaving and he said: 'Don't you go now and make a fool of me,' so threateningly I sat back down. Danny and Chrissie left, and Wayne walked off leaving me alone at the table. Pat* (a friend of mine from high school days) *called me over. I didn't get up. Instead, I waved him over, and Wayne saw me doing that, was furious and ran over and sat down between us. I kept talking to Pat so Wayne got up and said: 'Leave my woman alone.' Pat said: 'I'm only talking to her.' #*

Wayne left and I ran after him rather than be left alone at the venue. His panel van was parked near the police station and I tried to open the door while he sat inside the car. He wouldn't let me in so I banged on the door and he was furious, he jumped out and pushed me onto the road and I lost my shoe. Two policemen pulled up and one took Wayne aside and reprimanded him for disturbing the peace and almost charged him with PCA (now referred to as DUI, driving under the influence). *The other policeman asked me if I was okay and did I want a lift home as I was crying and he asked me my name and Wayne's. Instead of accepting his offer of a lift, Wayne and I walked to Tattersalls* (his idea to remove us from the police presence) *so that he'd hopefully, I was thinking, calm down. As soon as we sat down he wouldn't let up about me being a 'slut' and that I would have taken that guy (Pat from the 21st) home if he hadn't been there and that was it for us, he wanted out. He bought me a drink and said: 'Enjoy it, it's the last one you'll get from me because you'll be my ex-girlfriend tomorrow.' This drunk beside us repeated everything Wayne said to me so I went outside and Wayne came out yelling: 'If you don't come back in right now, you're worth nothing.'* (He was continually about-facing, sometimes as in the above scenario, within minutes. He'd say he wanted to split up and while I digested this he'd turn around and say he wanted me to stay and couldn't stand being without me. These conversations left me in a constant state of agitation and confusion but as was always the case I'd acquiesce to whatever he decided rather than think for myself, something I was by now incapable of doing.) # *I went back in and he again started arguing with me about being a slut and spat in my face so I walked out and sat near the Flye Inn crying. Wayne walked past calling me a harlot, he still wanted to argue and wouldn't leave me alone so I got a cab home and he followed me in his car. Narene was in bed when Wayne came in and he started smashing my coffee service and broke Narene's antique plate and salt and pepper shakers in the process. He pulled me into the bedroom and threw me around the room and I kept grabbing him to stop myself hitting the walls and he fell on the floor, so did I. He got up and kicked me repeatedly in the chest cutting it with his boot then picked me up and threw me across the bed and grabbed my neck and bashed my head into the brick wall three times all the while keeping his hands around my throat squeezing and I thought my head was split and started crying and yelling and my ankle was cut and bleeding everywhere. Wayne was furious still and kept pushing his hand into my face and eyes which gave me black eyes and a split lip which swelled up straight away. I punched him to get him away then he grabbed my neck and really started strangling me and said: 'I'm going to kill you, you bitch,' then: 'We're both going to be dead by the morning. I'm going to kill you bitch,' and it was a nightmare because he kept saying it so venomously and wouldn't let go of my neck. I was terrified thinking that I wasn't going to get out of this alive. I was so desperate and starting to black out knowing that if I didn't do something now he wasn't going to stop strangling me so I somehow got my knees up under his arms and kneed him in the stomach and fought free and screamed out for Narene rushed into her bedroom hysterical then we went into the kitchen. She said she'd been too scared to come out of her bedroom. I was shaking and babbling and Wayne rushed out and screamed: 'You fucking bitch, you're insane,' and went back into the bedroom. I lay on the lounge and was too dumb to talk. When Narene went to bed I went to the toilet and threw up.*

Please note that some of the entries in this book, such as the one above, lack grammatical structure however they need to be faithfully reproduced as they were originally chronicled. This technique of writing, I hope, conveys the desperation I felt both during and after each abusive episode as well as the absolute need I had at the time to vomit the words onto paper before incidents festered.

Sunday 4th May

Wayne got up at 7am and said: 'Are you going to work?' (I had found Wayne a cleaning job with a cleaning contractor in town and occasionally worked alongside him to earn a little money) and I said: 'With this face?' (I had a split and bruised lip, bruises on the side of my face and all over my neck from his fingers and a cut on my face too. My head had lumps on it and my eyes were black) so he went back into the bedroom and slammed the door then came out and said: 'Thanks for ruining last night for me and today,' and left. He came back at 9.30 and said: 'If you don't go to work with me, it's finished between us,' then: 'Do you still want to go out with me?' to which I said no and he sat staring at me and said: 'I guess I overreacted last night.' Carl (friend of Wayne's and by now a work colleague of his) *came and I went to the toilet with diarrhoea and I vomited then went to work with them and stopped in at Wayne's parents for aspirin. They were angry with Wayne for hitting me then Pam* (his mother) *said they'd put him in a 'loony bin' soon for slapping me around the face where you can see the bruises. Later Wayne apologised and was very talkative trying to make it up to me. He said he didn't realise how dependent he was on me until last night and couldn't leave because he didn't want to lose me and if I'd gone away he would have come after me. He also said he likes to be dominated by women and that I'm indecisive and can't commit myself to anything and I should dominate him more. Whatever that means?*

I later understood that in Wayne's eyes being dominated by a woman partly meant being sexually dominated by a woman. Sex with him was forced upon me, yet Wayne complained that I was not forceful enough during the act!

For many days after the above violence, the little of my old self still remaining, recoiled whenever Wayne tried to pretend that nothing had happened that wasn't a result of the way I'd acted while we were downtown. All blame for his loss of control was directed towards me. Because he was so adamant that I'd caused his violence by my actions, I was eventually persuaded that if I changed, the abuse would never occur again. As I now reflect on this I am appalled that I did not at the time examine the true meaning behind his compulsion to inflict such violence. Instead, I warped the incident's significance so that I was in my mind more the abuser than he was. How had I been reduced to thinking in this manner, so quickly?

Wednesday 11th June

We moved into the new flat in Sunset Avenue in Alka Springs (I from the unit I'd shared with Narene, he from his parents' backyard) and I spent all day unpacking and organising the furniture while Wayne went to work. When he got home he yelled at me for forgetting to go to the electricity commission earlier after he'd rang them and said I'd be there. They put the electricity on anyway irrespective of my absence at their office so Wayne's annoyance was irrelevant. Then Wayne said: 'I'll do everything myself from now on,' so I stomped upstairs and he called me an arsehole. #

Thursday 19th June

We went to the Flye Inn tonight then Wayne brought friends of his back to the house and he got uptight because he thought I was trying to win on to any guy I talked to. It got so I couldn't talk to anyone without getting filthy looks from him so I went upstairs and thought everything was okay until Wayne came up at 3.30am and screamed at me. # He said I was a slut and flirted with everyone tonight and I let him down and he wanted me out, then suddenly he hugged me and said: 'I don't know how I can hug you but I love you,' then he switched mood # and wanted to kill me. He threw me around the room and I nearly broke my elbow and there were bruises all over my legs from being kicked and even though I cried and screamed and was in pain, he was selfish and could only think of himself and wouldn't listen to my explanations so I screamed at him and ran downstairs. He came after me and carried me upstairs and yelled: 'You go anywhere and I'll kill you.' He tried to choke me, kept hitting me and I got up and he chased me around with his fists up saying: 'I'll hit you properly.' I was petrified and when he threw me on the bed I pretended I was asleep until I thought he was, hoping that would stop him hitting me. Later, I went to get up and he said: 'I'll go and find Tracy (old girlfriend) that's who I want. She won't let me down. I'll go downtown tomorrow night and get a fuck and bring her home and screw her in front of you.'

Friday 20th June

I was really resentful and not talking to Wayne and he said later: 'I'm sick of you being cold to me. What's in your mind?' I made him promise not to throw me around like that again and he said he wouldn't but I wonder if he'll keep that promise? # When we went to bed I turned my back on him before he had a chance to demand sex.

Saturday 21st June

Wayne thought we were getting on well but I was cold toward him every time I thought about what he'd done to me and I hated him. Meanwhile he's saying: 'Every couple has arguments. I hate you sometimes and could kill you, you hate me sometimes but we get over it ha.' # When we went to bed Wayne said: 'Aren't you going to make love to me?' but I went to sleep and next morning he said: 'I was waiting to see if you were going to make love to me but you didn't.' This was said plaintively as if he was perplexed and could see no reason for my withdrawal of sexual favours.

Friday 4th July

We were at the Grand when Narene and Peter came and sat at our table, and Narene was upset because she thought I didn't want to be friends anymore as I never visited her (only because Wayne kept me so busy that I didn't have a chance to see my friends). # Peter went off to talk to friends and Wayne and Narene talked, and when Peter came back he apparently got annoyed at Wayne for 'being too chummy with Narene', Wayne's explanation for his next actions. (I didn't hear what was said.) The bar closed just then and we left and ran into Peter and Narene at the back door. Wayne went to hit Peter and I grabbed him to stop that. Before I knew it, Wayne grabbed Peter and dragged him into the car park, hit him and threw him around and Peter had no chance to defend himself. A barman came out and broke it up. When we got home I took my stockings off to get changed and Wayne started an argument saying that I never seduced him and if I didn't start being more of a woman he'd go and sleep with one, so I had to put my stockings back on and have sex # even though I was upset about him fighting with my best friend's boyfriend.

I didn't see Narene again for 12 years. She wouldn't talk to me until I left 'that maniac' as she called Wayne.

Wednesday 30th July

I'd been at work all day so had to go downtown after I'd finished to do some food shopping and when I got home, exhausted, Wayne of course yelled at me for not getting home sooner and wanted to know who I'd seen and where I'd been in a really interrogating tone. He's so possessive. #

Thursday 31st July

I was supposed to be home before Wayne went back to work at 1.20 but didn't get out of the hairdressers until 1.30 and when I got home Wayne had gone back to work so I knew I was in for it when he got back at 4.30. He was furious that I wasn't home at lunchtime even though I was a lousy 10 minutes' late home. # He came home later then went back to work at 5.30 after screaming at me for an hour. I felt so depressed that he didn't notice my hair. He's never looking at me unless I'm providing a 'screw' or whatever he wants. When he got home he was still furious so we didn't talk, then when we went up to bed, he said: 'I don't love anyone but myself, I don't get the high with you I got with other chicks in the past. I've never felt that high with you.' I said: 'Well, what are you doing with me then?' and went downstairs and he screamed: 'You get back up here you fucking bitch,' so I did and he said: 'Go ahead and sook just because I said I don't love you.' Later he said: 'I do love you. You'll have to believe that I wouldn't know what to do if you left.' # I know it's a lukewarm love if that, otherwise he wouldn't be so critical of my looks and say things like: 'I used to do everything for Sharon (an ex-girlfriend who committed suicide). *I was in love with her nonstop everyday not like with you, I'd give her everything.' He makes me crazy.*

Such was the degree of madness I experienced at the time that I could consider anything Wayne did stemmed from even a 'lukewarm love' and not realising that his behaviours resulted from a complete lack of any form of love for me. Alarmingly and also indicative of my madness was my inability to understand that his behaviours raised serious concerns for his mental well-being and my safety.

Friday 1st August

Today he said: 'I think I am in love with you and want to marry you,' but all I could think was I wished I didn't know him, he thinks I'm a fool (and I kept feeding that impression).

Just prior to this declaration my previous boyfriend Michael had called me on the phone. He'd been trying for months, he said, to get my contact number and that he wanted to renew our friendship. He asked me if I was happy with Wayne and said that he was still single. Wayne of course was listening to my end of the conversation and, realising who I was talking to, snatched the phone off me and yelled at Michael never to call me again. I believe his thinking that he may have had competition for my affection pre-empted his declaration of marriage. After this call, Wayne screened my calls by being the first to answer the phone every time it rang. # As we both worked all day and were usually at home together, I rarely had the luxury of privacy while on the phone, nor were my conversations lengthy as Wayne would time my calls and tell me, in no uncertain terms, to hang up after only a few moments talking to others (mainly family by this stage as the majority of my friends had lost contact). God forbid that I did not devote my entire existence to attending to his conversational requirements alone.

Saturday 2nd August

We went to the RSL and Wayne made me wear a tight white dress and high heels then yelled at me outside the club for flirting and eyeing off 'every guy in the place' and punched my arm. Later he took my hand as we walked home and said: 'You're the first girl who's ever been able to talk me out of a bad mood from jealousy.'

Wednesday 6th August

Wayne wouldn't give me a lift to work even though he had the day off so I got a cab and he said: 'I wish you'd hurry up and leave for work I can hardly wait to be alone.' I rang him from work and woke him so he was angry and when I simply asked if he wanted extra work cleaning the motel windows he screamed: 'Mind your own business. I can find my own work,' but apologised later as he wanted someone (me) to talk to. He didn't like the pie I made for dinner, it was 'shit'. He'd do the shopping from now on because I had 'the worst taste in the world'. He said I was like my mother in that respect and would never find a guy to stay with me. I hated him at that moment.

Saturday 16th August

At the Gentlemen's Club, Wayne said he wouldn't mind marrying me then Chris (friend of Wayne's) came over and talked to Wayne and brought up that night of the 21st when we'd left early. Wayne was furious, thinking he'd been made a fool of that night and here it was being discussed again. We went out in the foyer because the club was closing, then started walking up to the main street and Wayne pushed me around near the hardware place. I fell and hit my head on the footpath, then this guy came over and stepped in to stop Wayne kicking me. I ran back to the foyer crying and a barman rang a cab and I got in and ran into Wayne running to it so I let him in to stop him making a scene out on the road. We went home and as we got to the door he was yelling at me and manhandling me saying: 'Just you wait until we get inside, you'll be sorry. You've made a fool of me again and I won't put up with it.' I was scared by the creepy tone of his voice and ran up the road and got as far as next door and he came tearing after me and tackled me in full flight down onto the road and I split the front of my head on the bitumen and the neighbour heard us and came out and Wayne was punching me over and over in the face and hitting the back of my head into the roadway and throwing me all over the road. The neighbour went back inside and got dressed and came out and Wayne was still hitting me and punching me in the face every time I went to sit up to get away from him. I split my head again and had gravel rash all over my legs and arms and face and Wayne fell and split his lip while he was trying to punch my face and he thought his teeth were knocked out and we were covered in blood and lost heaps and my hands were covered in it. I had gravel rash up and down my legs and arms and I was in agony and hysterical so the guy drove us to casualty and they gave me stitches first and Wayne said Aborigines had hit us. He rang his mother, she picked us up from the hospital and we slept in his parent's spare room. They talked to Wayne about it and he said: 'I love her. I don't know why I did it.' Wayne came into the bedroom and asked if I was leaving him and I didn't answer so he cracked up and said: 'I'll go and get Tracy (the ex-girlfriend and supposedly the 'love of his life' as he'd often told me) *she'd come crawling back even if I did hit her.' He was furious and his parents had to calm him down.*

The entry above is difficult for me to read written as it is in a hurried, frantic way, as if the mere effort of writing about what happened was almost as traumatising as the event, and needed to be recorded as quickly as possible. It was just as quickly packed away into my subconscious where it was less painful. Throughout my time with Wayne I did not examine how I felt. By not looking deeply at the abuse and its deleterious effects on my mental stability, I was abusing myself almost as much as Wayne was abusing me.

Deborah Thomson

Sunday 17th August

Woke up with a raging headache and backache and couldn't stand up without being sick and giddy and Wayne said to his parents: 'She's ok,' but his mother took me to outpatients and I kept throwing up so they gave me a needle to stop that. I had blurred vision and was so dizzy I couldn't sit up. Pam left and I lay in outpatients for five hours then they took me up to West Wing to a bed.

Monday 18th August

Was woken at 5am for a shower. My face is puffed up like a bullfrog with two black eyes and bruises all over my face and my hair still covered in blood. I could hardly walk and they're checking me every two hours and my eyes were sluggish to the light shining in from the doctor's torch. Later the next-door neighbour from last night came in and I had to ask if I knew him as I didn't remember him. He asked if we fought like that all the time. He was a counsellor at Helpman House and I think he wanted to rehabilitate us as he was asking what I wanted to do and if he could help. He'd called the police to our house the next day after it happened as he thought I'd want to press charges but Wayne was pretending to be asleep (he later told me in a smug self-satisfied voice as if he'd gotten one over the police) when they came and I was in hospital, so neither of us was interviewed. I said I didn't want to cause trouble because that would make Wayne even angrier. I was scared and just wanted it all to go away. I thought that if I stopped Wayne from getting into trouble with the police that the whole thing would disappear. The counsellor left finally and Wayne came and was furious about the police. He said they came into it because I was in hospital and shouldn't be and I shouldn't have run up the road that night and involved others. I had to go home now so he 'wouldn't be alone to think', so I got the doctor to come and check me before discharge. The doctor didn't want to let me go as I could barely stand while he checked me over. They wanted me to stay another day but I talked them out of it. Bought Panadol on the way home and Barry (Wayne's Dad) said I was part of the family and if it happened again to come to him and he'd talk to Wayne to make sure there wasn't a repeat incident. (After later abusive incidents I refrained from going to Barry as I sensed, rightly, that he would not be of much help in changing the violent course Wayne was following.) Wayne kept on assuring me for the next couple of days that it wouldn't happen again. # I believed him. I stayed home from work for a week as I had so many bruises on my face and didn't want work mates to see them. Wayne's mother rang my boss to get me time off, saying that I had fallen down the stairs in my home irrespective of her knowing the truth. I continued the lie by telling Mum the same thing when I called her.

When I returned to work I still had bruises on my face and one work friend took me aside, showed me scars on her neck from her abusive ex-husband and said: 'I know when I see a beaten woman and I can tell you that I don't believe you fell down any stairs.' I denied that Wayne had caused my injuries as I was embarrassed about all that had happened and I just wanted to forget about it. She said she was sorry that I wouldn't admit the truth and that if I needed to talk she'd listen.

She was the only person at that time who was genuinely shocked by my injuries urging me to source outside support.

Having herself been abused at the hands of her husband, her antennae were up, enabling her to see when another was suffering in the same way. This was the second person to encourage me to bring the abuse into the open but yet again I kept everything within.

Wednesday 26th August

Wayne wanted to have sex tonight and got really uptight when I said no. Then he said he's sick of the same 'hole' anyway and wouldn't mind other chicks but didn't chase them. Wow that's good of him?!

Friday 24th October

We discussed how it was when Wayne first began contract cleaning and that I hadn't worked with him in the beginning. I said: 'What if I didn't now work with you, where would you be?' He said: 'I didn't need you before. I got along well and I don't need you now,' then he apologised for arguing later when he got back from work. While we were at The Octopus to buy fish for dinner he asked me to buy two pieces and I thought he meant for the both of us not just for him. When we got home and saw it was two not three pieces (two for him, one for me), he screamed at me until I said: 'Have mine as well. I don't want it.' He became really violent and shoved me around and screamed: 'You eat it or I'll jam it up your arse,' then later he said he was going out to get another woman which would be 'easy to do'. Within two minutes he did an about-face and said to me it wouldn't be fair not taking me out too! He said: 'I'm the luckiest guy in town and I like taking you out to show you off. Guys notice you when I'm with you and it's good.'

But then in a bad mood he'll say: 'You're too stroppy and useless,'
and: 'I have to find a young chick to screw, you are worn around
the edges and don't look young anymore.' # Went to bed and had
sex of course. I can't believe he gets so upset over something so
mundane as pieces of fish. #

Tuesday 25th November

Terrible day, I've been on edge around Wayne all morning. He was
uptight about going to work in the afternoon so while he was gone
I rushed around cleaning up and cooking so that he wouldn't be
angry when he got back. I was still at it when he got home and we
hardly talked then I put dinner on the table and he said he didn't
want it. I went to put it in the oven and he screamed to leave it. I
put it back on the table and he said: 'This is shit,' and threw the
plate at me and everything else on the table. It was a huge mess
and he made me clean it up.

Sunday 30th November

Woke up screaming from nightmares in my sleep and accidentally
woke Wayne and he grabbed my neck and pushed my head into
the pillow and said: 'Shut the fuck up, you're crazy.' I'm crazy?
He then said: 'You're a cunt of a person to sleep with and we need
separate beds.' I'm so tired of everything.

'I'm so tired of everything' was a gross understatement. For
a more accurate description of my state of mind I should have
written that I was sick to my soul from constantly being on
tenterhooks in Wayne's presence, waiting for the inevitable
outburst from him. I cannot reiterate enough that despite my
soul sickness, I felt that I had no other option than to stay

and through my staying, discover the key to eliminating his abuse. It may have been sheer stubbornness or an altruistic determination to make him happy, but however my reasoning worked, it was based on the premise that Wayne was mentally stable. I did not understand the dynamics of domestic violence nor the seriousness of Wayne's mental issues and spent much of our relationship numb with shock. I was essentially tilting at windmills thinking that I could make a positive difference to his state of mind.

Friday 5th December

Wayne hadn't taken me out in ages so we went out tonight and he complained about having to take me out. I hardly talked to anyone because when I did he got uptight and angry. # When we got home he started yelling that I was ungrateful, he spent money on me all the time and paid for everything, he had to drive me to work. He said: 'When I do take you out, you won't talk to my friends, you're a snob and a bitch and a flirt and if you hadn't been there tonight I could have screwed Michelle.' I couldn't work out what was happening and why he was turning on me and I tried to ask him what he meant and he screamed: 'Shut up, I'm never taking you out again,' and went to sleep.

Here is another example of a crucial warning sign. The abuser has an uncanny knack of manipulating reality, turning an argument into an indictment of your behaviours causing you to believe you're at fault, leaving you more confused and wondering how the discussion had degenerated into an attack on yourself.

Friday 12th December

Wayne was at Impies after work and rang me and said to get dressed and get a cab there. We sat near the juke box and Phil (friend of Wayne's) came over and talked to us. When he left, Wayne said that he was sleazing all over me but that was alright, it didn't worry him. 'It's good for the ego,' he said, 'I've got what he wants.' After saying this, he suddenly became angry and spat on me and swore at me. # I tried to calm him down then he turned around in a matter of minutes and said: 'No wonder guys are all over you, you're gorgeous.' For the rest of the night he had digs at me saying I was a dumb broad, then he left me alone to hit on Michelle so I caught a cab home. Wayne got back at 3am and swore when he tried to wake me and I pretended I was asleep.

When Wayne wasn't having rapid mood changes, he was denigrating my intelligence, my values, my views and my physical appearance. When I'd defend myself against his observations, he'd deny that he'd said such things and that I was hallucinating. This conversation would occur between us so often, that I became convinced that I was indeed hallucinating or I'd be so confused that I would be left wide open to his manipulation. It was a form of psychological abuse.

Friday 19th December

He thought I went to turn the alarm off this morning and we'd be late to work so he started screaming at me and threw me off the bed saying: "I'm leaving you, you're useless.'

His overreaction to innocuous things was also mental abuse. His attacks left me emotionally abused and constantly on edge waiting for the next outburst. I knew that absolutely anything could set him off but I had no idea what that 'anything' would be.

We had by now moved from Sunset Avenue into a house in Joseph Street and things between us had not improved. Instead our relationship had deteriorated with Wayne exerting more control over my life than ever.

Thursday 25th December

Mum had travelled from the Gold Coast in Queensland, Grandma and Grandpop from the Central Coast in our state to stay at the house over Christmas. It was the first Christmas I'd spent with all three family members in four years. The visit was, for me, an event looked forward to eagerly. However, for Wayne it was very stressful as he was, he told me, very much afraid that my family would talk me into leaving Alka Springs. He'd sensed during other meetings with Mum that she didn't approve of our relationship. Wayne's stress set the scene for what became a Christmas ruined by extreme rudeness on his part. His abuse toward my family was just another attempt to destroy any bond I had with people in my life other than him. #

I don't know what started the fight but Mum told Wayne to get stuffed and he told her to get fucked, she ran into the bedroom crying. It was awful. Rick (my brother) phoned to wish us Merry Christmas and Mum told me later that he hated Wayne and thought he was using me as a personal slave. Only Grandpop talked to him all that day because he is deaf and couldn't hear what Wayne was saying to everyone else in the house. Mum asked me how I could live with such an illiterate pig, animal, a chauvinist and country hick. I was thinking I DON'T KNOW but couldn't tell her that because it would feel like I'm a failure if I can't make the only long-term relationship I've ever had work, then have to go out on my own. No one else would want me, they never have before, so what would be different? (Such was my thinking, so low was my self-esteem.) I had to make this work and show everyone they were wrong about Wayne.

Friday 26th December

Wayne worries Mum will talk me into leaving him so tells me I should stick with his family and not see mine. #

Saturday 27th December

Mum and I argued because she wanted to go out and I didn't because Wayne was angry about that and didn't want me to. I knew if I did there'd be trouble. Mum went out into the lounge room and she and Grandma said they'd take the videos back and get others. Wayne said: 'It's an idiot box until there are videos in it,' and Mum said 'what a clever boy Wayne.' He yelled at her and said: 'You're a joke for a mother,' and they really started in at each other so I ran out back and Mum and Grandma came out after me. Mum said: 'How could you let him speak to me like that?' and Grandma said: 'Get rid of him.' Listening to them I felt cornered. I knew they were right but I wasn't ready to leave Wayne so I screamed in frustration and raced back inside. As they left to walk downtown, Wayne went to the front door and screamed: 'Don't come back.' After they'd gone I walked around the block feeling sick and stressed. When I came back Wayne said: 'We get closer together when there's a crisis, we'll get through this together.' He considered the whole thing sorted but I felt disgusting.

Somehow, I knew that by allowing him to talk to my family like that and choosing to stay with him, some sort of corner had been turned and I could never go back. Mum later hugged me and we talked but she was still furious and said she was worried about me staying with the animal, saying that he needed help because he was manic depressive.

Looking back, I can now clearly see a pattern whereby, whenever my family or friends were with me, Wayne would find an excuse to try and drive a wedge between those I loved and myself so that I would become inexorably, increasingly isolated and under his control. At the time, I did not see that his actions were designed to achieve this. Instead I felt that I was doing something to hurt him by not wanting to spend the entire time alone with him and so I tried to rectify the situation by relinquishing my friends and family. For that I felt and still feel incredibly guilty, but I had to assuage Wayne's 'hurt' at all costs. Reluctantly his family and friends became the family I'd lost. He permitted me to see my family only rarely and I allowed him to dictate when and where this occurred. Co-dependency occurs where the abuser uses the abused for his own gains and the abused, the worse they are treated, assumes greater responsibility to right the wrongs, thinking that this will increase theirs and the abuser's self-esteem and worth. Both abused and abuser consider their roles as that of saviour and master respectively, believing that they need each other to fulfil these roles.

I stayed with him even after he'd methodically isolated me from all my friends as well as from every family member who had the extreme misfortune to meet Wayne. It didn't matter what he said or did to others and to me; there seemed to be this inevitable path I was on that I couldn't avoid, a trajectory that propelled me to a place I didn't want to go to but couldn't avoid: running scared—scared of him, but also of being alone—then feeling that immobilization was my best option. I was alone in a bubble and too ashamed to tell anyone what was happening, especially after having moved in with him. To leave was unthinkable. I wasn't strong enough. Why? I didn't know. Indecision and fear, whenever I thought about getting out, prevented my actually doing so. That gave him the control that cemented our sick bond. Deferring as I did to his wishes was a form of 'temporary' insanity that lasted for over seventeen years.

1987

I have copied fewer diary entries for 1987. This is not because less happened that was of a violent nature but rather because so many similar events occurred daily. Were I to include all entries where violence occurred, the sheer volume may put the reader at risk of becoming as immune to the violence as I was.

Wayne and I bought a contract cleaning business for $5000. Although it became very lucrative for us, it was another brick in the wall binding us together and one more reason for me to strive harder to be the woman he wanted. Somehow, I felt there was more to lose should our relationship end and so I did what I thought was needed to keep us together.

Saturday 10th January

Again, a hard day's work. After it was over I was beside the fridge when the walls slid out towards me, I suffered a bad case of vertigo and nearly fainted. When I told Wayne, he couldn't have cared less, said I was a wimp and a bludger who couldn't stand a bit of work. # (At that stage, I was doing at least 10 hours of cleaning over three shifts a day.) *We went to St Peter's College* (one of many of Alka Spring's private high schools and our major cleaning contract) *for the afternoon shift. He was alright until I brought* up the argument from earlier regarding him thinking I couldn't work. He screamed at me: 'Shut up, you fucking bitch. I'll leave you if you don't get your act together.' After work, he talked me into going over to Dave's (friend of Wayne's) place. I don't know why I went as Wayne was either rude to me or ignored me the whole time we were there. #

Tuesday 13th January

After the morning's work, we went home for a break. Wayne had Bourbon and became uptight when I mentioned Tracy his ex and knowing that I was second best to her. My words made him furious and he belted Joey (his beloved dog) then smashed his Bourbon glass, threw the coffee table across the room, rushed at me then ran out the door. He came back later to get me for work and said: 'Don't you know that I love you. I'll never let you go, never, so watch out.' # We went to work and nothing more was said.

Wednesday 14th January

Wayne brought up yesterday's incident and got angry again and yelled: 'I'm going to hell and back with you,' and came at me so I slammed the door in his face. He screamed that he was leaving me saying: 'You're no support and fucking useless,' then he almost immediately calmed down and said: 'What would I do without you? You're the best a man could ever have.' #
I can't fathom his moods.

Friday 16th January

Wayne said he loved me because I didn't try to change him unlike other girlfriends. (What was strongly implied was that aside from not changing him, I also obeyed him, waited on him, served him and generally lived my life through and for him.) *Steve* (friend of Wayne's) *rang asking us to come over his place and Wayne said no, that he had drunk too much so Steve said he'd pick us up. Wayne told me I wasn't going so we started arguing and he grabbed me and half strangled me and said quietly: 'What do you want me to do, tell me, I won't go if you tell me not to.' I couldn't say anything as I was choking and my head was spinning. He walked out and when he got back home I was in bed. This seemed to infuriate him so he smashed the bedroom mirror and bed lamp. He was so full of adrenalin he managed to drag the mattress off the bed and across the room with me on it. He threw himself on me trying to suffocate me, then he collapsed crying. He staggered out to the lounge room blubbering: 'Here's your man, a blithering idiot, see what you do to me. I'm afraid I'll hurt you, the woman I love, if I don't get under control. You have to stop fucking my head up.' He left again and I wish he'd done that in the first place instead of smashing the place up.*

Never mind trying to suffocate me! In those days, I was more concerned for the furniture than for my own health.

Thursday 5th February

Finished the morning work at 10.30am and rang home to tell Wayne I was going shopping. No one was there so I went downtown and did the shopping then went home. Wayne had left an abusive note saying: 'Sick of looking for you, Steve and I are going to the Bowling Club without you,' so I had to sit at home nervously waiting for him until 1.30pm when they came back. They'd ended up playing tennis instead of snooker at the Club.

They'd gone to pick me up from work before that and I wasn't there so they'd driven everywhere according to Wayne, looking for me. Naturally he thought I was off 'doing something sleazy' # and he called me a whore and screamed at me and shook me in front of Steve who had to sit through it all. Later he came in and apologised because Steve said he'd better.

Monday 16th February

Wayne yelled at me, called me a dumb bitch because he couldn't find the Visine. He blamed me and said: 'I'm getting sick of you being so stupid,' and I said: 'You're just hating me more now than you did before, that's all.' Steve came over and Wayne was really friendly to me while he was there. #

His friends, I think, had no idea of Wayne's capability of abusing me because he exercised such self-control over his behaviour towards me when others were present. Wayne was known as a 'brawler' when out at night but this fighting was accepted by those who knew him, being seen simply as typical masculine behaviour, even behaviour to look up to. Such aggressiveness, when displayed in seemingly appropriate contexts such as on the sports field or with mates in the pub, seems to be accepted as part of being male by society which often turns a blind eye to it. Yet so often those who are happy to 'bash' others in a street environment tend to bring the aggressiveness into the home as well. Abusers appear to lack an off switch unless having one works in their favour, or any knowledge of acceptable ways to rid themselves of the heightened anger they feel internally and exhibit externally.

Wednesday 8th April

Letter from Mum saying I shouldn't be living with Wayne, he's not right for me. After work at St Peter's, we dropped in to his parents to pick up our dogs and Pam (Wayne's mother) was drunk. Damian (Wayne's younger brother) argued with Wayne asking him to do something about her drinking. Wayne told him to fuck off and hit him twice and gave him a black eye.

Wednesday 15th April

Working at St Peter's and while Wayne was cleaning the girl's toilets I emptied the vacuums, came back after that and asked Wayne what he wanted me to do now. He yelled: 'I already told you to do the senior toilets,' and when I said: 'I didn't hear you earlier,' he thought I was back-chatting and screamed at me and threw his mop at me. It hit me in the face and he told me to 'fuck off and leave him alone'. We argued when we got home and I thought: 'What am I doing with this bastard?' He half-apologised later for the mop.

Thursday 7th May

Even though he hasn't worked in the morning all week and I have, he expects me to work all afternoon with him and it wouldn't hurt him to do it alone for once when I have a cold but oh no, I have to help him. We had a fight in the science labs (while cleaning them) while he was replacing the fluorescent light bulbs and he threw part of the fitting at me. It hit me just below the eye and cut my face so I ran out to the car and of course he came out and made me go back to work. He didn't say sorry for going at me for nothing, so I was mad at him but he still expected sex later. #

Sunday 24th May

*I yelled out 'get away' in my sleep and woke up and Wayne said:
'Get fucked, I'll get away all right.' He became angry, got out of
bed and said: 'Get fucked,' again, then: 'You can all get nicked,'
and I said: 'What did I do?' He was sarcastic and said: 'Of course
you wouldn't know and of course you did nothing wrong.' When
he came home from work he started arguing again, saying he
didn't believe me when I told him that I was asleep while saying
get away and he screamed that I was a stupid whore.*

So often during arguments Wayne would confuse me to
the point where I'd blame myself for the argument or I'd
believe his convoluted explanations for why he was angry to
begin with. His psychological abuse, given the brain-washing
element inherent in his arguments, was in many ways more
traumatic and hurtful than any other form of abuse that he
threw at me. It stayed in my mind longer and had a greater
negative effect on my sense of self.

The one thing more hurtful than the psychological abuse
was Wayne's complete lack of remorse regardless of what abuse
he inflicted on me. On the contrary, he would in most cases
following each incident, transform from being a screaming
and violent individual to one who was passive and congenial.
He'd seemingly forget what had just transpired and expected
me to act as he did after an abusive episode: business as usual.
This about-face caused me great confusion and despair,
allowing me no time to digest the violence (until later when
I was alone, by which time I'd repressed the incident). Rather,
I attempted to rationalise his actions, telling myself that I
was exaggerating the level of brutality and that what I'd just

experienced was not as significant as I'd thought and felt it to be during the abuse. This was secondary abuse and was equally as devastating as the initial assault. I still struggle with the trauma initially induced by his lack of acknowledgement of any wrongdoing at the time of the attacks.

Sunday 28th June

Wayne talked about how Dave and Marge (friends of his) were newly married and that Dave had confided in Wayne that he was now stuck with her and tired of her. I said he (Wayne) had just as bad an attitude towards women and in the car, we argued about what I'd said and he yelled: 'Get out you slut, no you won't get out, you want to stay and make my life a misery.' Later he about-faced # and said: 'I'm learning to think of both of us, it's a responsibility a relationship and I'm looking forward to it and having a kid.' He was very self-congratulating for having arrived at this conclusion.

If I had been thinking straight or even with a little capacity for reflection I would have seen Wayne's pattern, since we'd been together, of enforcing his own world view on me. He had been the one to force our relationship into a partnership, to move in together, marry, work together in business, live where we lived and now have children. I would agree with each decision that he imposed, convinced as I was of contributing to the choices he made for the both of us and of having some influence on how our lives unfolded. In reality, I was simply allowing myself to move to his beat. Doing this was easier as time passed by and self-reflection and thoughtful examination of where my life was heading became almost non-existent.

Deborah Thomson

Saturday 5th September

Worked all morning at the Grand Hotel as usual. Depressed all afternoon and had to help Wayne clean the library carpets. (We had the cleaning contract for the Alka Springs City Council and as part of that, the library contract.) *That took us four hours before we had to do the night run* (of cleaning contracts). *I went and did the shopping in the last hour and as I was leaving the library I guess I didn't open the back door as quickly as Wayne wanted me to so he pushed me to the ground and spat on me. # That really improved my self- esteem for the day.*

Friday 30th October

Wayne became angry and started arguing with me in the lounge room and he threw the calculator at me. It hit me in the arm and that hurt, bruises came up later. I am so sick of him throwing things at me that I got up to hit him but didn't. He went out for the night then came home and we had sex.

Saturday 31st October

We were in bed and Wayne said: 'I'll have to talk to Megan (my boss at work) *because you'll let her walk all over you,' and we argued and he screamed at me that I was a weak bitch. I went into the spare bedroom to sleep and he came in, dragged me back into bed and said: 'I didn't mean you were weak, just quietly spoken and we can't let her* (boss) *or anything come between us because I'm never letting you go.' We then went into the lounge room, watched TV and all was well as far as he was concerned. #*

Wayne had manipulation down to a fine art. He counter-intuitively made me feel interesting and cared for despite his actions to the contrary. I, in my state of low self-worth easily succumbed to his attentiveness and agreeableness, as he was simultaneously treating me like a doormat. Despite the violence; indeed because of the violence, I was determined to help him be happier. I felt this crushing, nullifying responsibility to make his life better. The speed with which I fell into the rut of being his keeper was frightening. It had to be my fault that he acted as he did. How could it be otherwise, I thought, when he, who was so popular with women and could have anyone he wanted, had chosen me over them? Therefore, if he was unhappy I must be the one making him so. Everyone around me—his mother, his friends and Wayne himself—told me I was lucky to have such an affectionate boyfriend and that I was to blame for his moods when they presented themselves. I was told I should do better and then Wayne wouldn't be so uptight.

After each violent episode, I'd tell myself that I'd know what to do to avoid a repeat incident; however, the triggers to his behaviour changed every time. I could never decipher the rules of this relationship *because there were no rules.* The absence of rules within the daily routine, the screaming at me, the violence and emotional manipulation all increased my confusion until I felt I was in the 'boiled frog analogy' in which the poor creature didn't notice the rising temperature until boiling point was reached, thus killing it. While at university I averaged credits and distinctions for my English, Sociology and Political Science assignments. My intelligence was not in question, yet as I read back over these events I imagine it would appear to the reader that I was the stupidest person alive to remain with Wayne. He told me often enough that I was an idiot and I am compelled to concur when I think of what occurred and how little I did to prevent it.

1988

Thursday 14th January

Wayne started arguing after work tonight and he started yelling, calling me a fucking slut so I said I wanted to leave him and he said: 'I'll put a chain on you so you can't leave, you can't scratch me out of your black book.'

Sunday 20th March

Awful, awful day. The car wasn't running properly so Wayne stopped at the saleyards and tried to fix it, got it going then we started arguing at Lamb Park and he threw the car keys away, then had to go looking for them. We went and cleaned the inside windows at the Civic Administration building and I accidentally locked the building keys in an office. Wayne came at me with the broom and said: 'I could murder you,' and he screamed that I was a stupid whore. The way he went on over an unintentional mistake infuriated me so I said I was leaving him and I meant it. He said: 'Good riddance to bad rubbish. I'll get you a bus ticket because you're going tomorrow.' Later he said: 'Well, what are you doing, are you leaving?' and I said: 'I've had enough. I have to leave.' He then said: 'I don't want you to go. You're the best thing that's happened to me in my life and I couldn't live without you.

I say anything in a temper but I don't mean it, we are made for each other. # You work so well and you look after me and it's not for work that I want you to stay it's because I love you, we're doing all this for our lives together. I could get another woman but I don't want one, I want you for the rest of my life. I've let work interfere but there's nothing as important as me and you.'

I'm so stupid, I stayed after hearing his declaration.

Wayne and I had bought property 38 kilometres out of Alka Springs so we moved from town to a rural setting. It was a beautiful area but it was isolated, with the nearest neighbours being on their own properties far from earshot of our house.

Friday 29th April

I locked the house keys in the cabin. (The house had not yet been built on the site; we lived in a small cabin for our first two years there.) *Luckily a window was open but then I left a bag in the shed and had to break in to retrieve it and so we were late to work. Wayne screamed at me until I couldn't stop crying at the front gate to the highway and when I got back in the car he said: 'You're a useless bitch and babbling idiot.' I said: 'You're a bastard and I hate you and I wish I had left you.' He spat at me and punched me and it hurt so I said: 'You pig,' and we didn't talk until we got back home after work. As soon as we were in bed he demanded sex.*

Friday 27th May

As we were driving to work all I said was: 'It's a bit early to go yet,' and Wayne screamed at me. Then this girl went past on a bike as we were going down the road and she smiled at Wayne. I said:

'If only she knew,' and he said: 'Maybe she wants to find out, you fucking bitch,' so I ignored him for the rest of the day. Of course, he made me masturbate him tonight saying: 'You never give me any. I'm not inhuman and I'll get it somewhere else if I don't get it here.'

Friday 24th June

The pregnancy test is positive and Wayne said that I'd given him what he most wanted and when we told his parents Pam said: 'I hope it's a girl, I've always wanted a little girl.' I don't know if I want to bring the baby up around Wayne but didn't have a chance to think of an alternative because straight away Pam said that we had to get married and she organised the priest for the wedding, that night.

Saturday 13th August

We married in Urindy with Mum audibly sobbing in her seat throughout the service, she was so upset by this wedding and at the reception. I didn't see much of any of my family and friends, everyone I knew gave up trying to get to me because they couldn't fight through his family and friends. When we went back to the motel after, about eight of his friends came and stayed until dawn and then we drove home and went to work all of the following day.

We did not have a honeymoon. To Wayne the wedding had been an excuse to drink with his friends and once the night was over anything as romantic as time spent together during a honeymoon was to him, merely a waste of money.

This wedding was a farce with both Wayne and I performing a duty according to his mother's notions of Catholicism, namely that a couple had to marry when the woman was expecting a child. Many years after the wedding Mum told me of a conversation Wayne and she had in the company of my family, where Mum had asked Wayne why one of his guests, an indigenous female, was wearing sunglasses inside at the reception. Wayne had blithely replied that the girl in question had been given two black eyes by her partner (Wayne's best friend at the time) the night before so that she wouldn't be tempted to approach other guys at the reception. Wayne went on to say that indigenous women expected their partners to beat them, that men were not men if they didn't abuse their women and were not respected if they didn't use their fists. Needless to say, my family were shocked at this not only because of the content of the conversation but that Wayne could so casually say these words, as if abuse was a normal thing between partners.

Friday 9th September

Wayne was in a foul mood and said: 'I have to do everything while you're pregnant.' He was cruel, said I was a bitch and he couldn't get on with me, I was hell to work with and would I care if he left me? I said: 'If that's what you want,' and he said: 'I'll kick you out as I'm not leaving the land. You go-what I say goes.' # After work, we had sex so that he'd stop arguing with me.

By this time, I was four months into the pregnancy.

Tuesday 4th October

Am still really small, I look fat more than pregnant. When I went into Buntings (a shop in town) carrying a load of groceries the woman behind the counter asked if I was pregnant and said that I shouldn't be doing the shopping like that, I should be taking it easy. When I later told Wayne what the woman said, he just told me that there was nothing he could do about it (the amount of work I was still doing), he had his own problems. I wonder if work is stopping me looking more pregnant. I eat enough but I'm not getting bigger.

Although violence continued to be a factor in our relationship, I maintained the fantasy of having a relationship free of abuse. I told myself that as we progressed the way other couples do in marriage, establishing financial security, building a home and so on, Wayne would come to value me. In reality Wayne's personality made it nearly impossible for him to conform to the dictates of societal norms or to truly feel love for me while my personality made it difficult for me to understand that in him.

Again, whatever my failings, nothing excuses the treatment meted out by him. This statement is self-evident but I felt at that time, that his behaviour was both my responsibility to change and caused by my actions, not his.

Counsellors have mentioned that abusers so often use the same phrases when verbally abusing that one could think they all went to the same school of domestic violence. Without diminishing the anguish it causes, it is easy to discern such abusive language when perpetrators continue to repeat things such as 'I didn't mean to ...', 'It was only a push, I didn't think she'd fall,' 'I wouldn't get angry if you didn't ...', 'You are so stupid, you make me ...' and one of the most common phrases: 'I'm not an abuser, it's not like I punch her.' Abusers tend to have similarities in personality with the majority contemptuous of other people and blaming those outside themselves for whatever is going wrong in their lives. Abusers tend to be narcissistic with an inflated sense of entitlement. They have often been over-indulged as children and believe that they are owed more from life than they receive. Understanding these factors could assist a person considering a relationship with an abuser (or potential abuser with a predilection to abuse) to reconsider their next step.

1989

Wednesday 18th January

Woke up with such a heavy feeling in my abdomen. Could hardly walk to the toilet and lost more fluid on the way there. On the way to town I had a terrible stitch in my left side then pain dragging in my stomach every ten minutes and the pains got stronger as the day wore on. Wayne and Damian went to the Tyson Street house to do the lawn (we had the Housing Commission houses cleaning contract) then Pam, Heather (an employee) *and I went up later to clean the house. Wayne went to St Peter's while we finished the place and I swept the paths outside while in labour. My contractions were three minutes apart so Pam drove over to St Peter's and told Wayne and he said that I had to keep cleaning until the house was finished as he was too busy doing what he was doing to take my place. I had to work for another hour with the most excruciating dragging pains imaginable. It felt as if my entire stomach was going to drop out onto the ground then by the time I got to the hospital the baby had locked into place and the contractions had stopped. My blood pressure was 140/110. The doctor said it was meant to be 128/75.*

Deborah Thomson

Monday 23rd January

Wayne came up in the morning. (I remained in hospital from the 18th January until the 3rd of February.) *He says he's depressed and hates it out there alone and needs a woman. He's been staying in town and going out every night for the company he says.*

Charmaine was born on the 27th January weighing 5 lb 9 and a half ounces, underweight for her body length.

Saturday 28th January

My blood pressure is still so high they won't let me go for a week. Pam is here all the time since the birth and makes me feel like I'm just a vessel for carrying her precious baby. Now that she's born Pam is abrupt with me and all over the baby who Wayne named Charmaine. She weighed at birth (as mentioned) 5lbs 9 and a half ounces, head circumference 32 cm, born at quarter past 6pm, 54 and one-half cm long, the longest baby in the ward and the lightest too. She is beautiful but I hardly get the chance to hold her, as soon as I do Pam grabs her and walks away.

Sunday 29th January

Wayne is too busy to visit but Pam came of course. Charmaine had been wide awake all day and I only just got her to sleep when Pam came and deliberately woke her. She wouldn't leave her alone (I'm going to have trouble with her over everything I want done for Charmaine, she is adamant in her own ideas of caring for a baby) *so much so that I told her I needed rest and to leave. After she left I couldn't get Charmaine to sleep again and the nurse and I tried to get her to feed for six hours. She cried all night and it was awful then at 4.30am the nurse took her to the nursery and gave her a bottle of formula.*

Saturday 25th March

Went to Gary's (Wayne's cousin Katrina was becoming engaged to Gary) engagement party and Wayne as usual raved to everyone else and ignored me and then he had the hide to be rude to me for talking to this man who was also talking to his mother. After dinner, we all went downstairs to dance and Wayne wouldn't, so Ralph (Wayne's uncle) got me up and Wayne was angry at me about that too. We argued all the way home then because I wouldn't have sex with him as I'm still recovering from Charmaine's birth, and we were sleeping in his parent's lounge room after all, he said: 'Fuck you I could go downtown and get a whore if you won't do it. I should have stayed single.' I felt so rotten I cried then he said: 'I love you and I always will.' His about-face left me gobsmacked. #

Monday 10th April

Terrible day rushing around plus I had to see Dr Wilco (who'd delivered Charmaine) who gave me an internal and said I had a virus which luckily is starting to heal, but I can't have intercourse at the moment. Wayne blames me for not having sex and says I'm holding out on him and won't even get dressed up for him. I'm so tired and stressed from rushing every day at work of course I'm not interested, even if he had been acting like a decent human being.

Saturday 22nd April

Work as usual, didn't get home until late afternoon, Barry came out and he and Wayne wormed the horses and cows and he left a couple of hours later. No one remembered it was my birthday until later tonight when I had to masturbate Wayne to 'celebrate'.

Monday 24th April

Wayne said how disappointed he was that we had a girl when his best friend Perry had just had his first, a boy. This friend told him when he visited Wayne that his girlfriend is coming to live with him soon from out west and she has a sister. Wayne said: 'Tell her to bring her sister.' He does that all the time in front of mates, makes out he can't wait to get his hands on some other woman as if I'm ugly and don't have enough sex with him. #

Thursday 27th April

Cleaned Alka Springs Regional Art Museum, rushed home, then had to go back in to town for the night work and Wayne hurried me to the front door of the cabin. I asked him not to push me so he opened then slammed the door in my face. He raised his fist to punch me and I said: 'Go on, give me an excuse to leave,' and he said: 'You don't need one, just get.' When he realised I was serious, he said: 'You'll get a bullet and I'll bury you where no one will find you. There are places out here I know where they'll never find you, and I'll just say you walked out and I don't know where you've gone. So be careful.' When we got home again we had sex.

Wednesday 3rd May

Wayne argued with me all day over nothing. # *He said I got on his nerves then he yelled and yelled because I left some work papers at the* Civic Administration *building (another major contract). They were in the car the whole time, we found out later. He yells at me for nothing; yet, Pam can't do a thing wrong. According to Wayne, I'm just 'alright on the day'. I listen to him and her constantly talking about how Charmaine and Wayne are alike and it hurts. I might as well not be her mother as far as they are all concerned. I'd leave if it wasn't for Charmaine. Nothing else is worth staying for but both Pam and Wayne have already said that Charmaine would never leave them, that if I left she'd stay with them. I believe that is exactly what would happen.*

Wednesday 17th May

Went to town and Pam had bought Charmaine more clothes and tried to hide them from me. She won't listen to me when I say that Charmaine's not ready for solids and she gave her a full jar of food. No wonder she's constipated and crying. Pam buys clothes for Charmaine when I say no and says Charmaine's looking more and more like Wayne and it's so obvious that I'm just a sitter for her baby. When I said something to Wayne about how I felt he just argued and yelled at me to 'stop nagging' him, then he expected sex when we got home from work.

Friday 19th May

Took Charmaine to the clinic this morning and they said she is one kilo too heavy for her age. I can't stop Pam overfeeding her; she does it behind my back while I'm working. She says over and over that when Wayne was five weeks old he was eating a full jar of food and having arrowroot biscuits softened in warm milk and it didn't damage him. Wayne refuses to listen to anything I say about rearing babies as his mother knows best and there's nothing wrong with the way he was brought up. When we got home we watched the movie *The Sting* and he fell asleep halfway through it as it was 'too slow' then woke up later and we had sex.

Wednesday 31st May

Another awful day of work. I cleaned the house in Maclean Street while Wayne started the lawn and carted rubbish out. The house was filthy of course. Went home for lunch at 12 then back at 1pm where I finished cleaning inside then raked the front and half of the back lawn, the hardest part of the house cleaning I think. Finished at 3, went back to Pam's and washed up then went on the night run of cleaning to St Peter's until 5.30, then the Civic Admin. until 7.30, the library until 10.30 then we drove home at 11.30pm. Wayne keeps saying that we're not getting on well, I've changed, I don't spoil him enough and that I'm too aggressive. He started on me tonight after we finally got home saying the same things, that I don't give him enough in bed and that he deserves to be spoilt with all he does for me. #

Thursday 13th July

We cleaned the art museum in the early morning, then this huge house in Brewery Lane, back to Pam's for lunch and I washed two loads of clothes and cleaning rags then back to work until 9 and home by 10pm. Wayne and I sat in the dining room and he started arguing about nothing in particular and screaming abuse at me. I'd had enough and slapped his face and he slapped me back and threw a full glass of Coke straight in my face and most of it went in my eyes. It really burned and that scared me because I thought I'd go blind. I was in shock and couldn't see; however, Wayne didn't care. How could he do that to me, not giving a damn when I was seriously scared for my eyesight? It was then that I realised that Wayne had no respect for me and that I had lost all self-respect for myself.

The reader may well ask why this relatively innocuous incident, compared to prior more violent episodes, illuminated the true state of things for me. I think it was the fact that he completely disregarded my welfare although I was convinced I had been blinded by the Coke he had deliberately thrown in my eyes. Even then, this potentially disastrous situation did not bring him to care.

By then, I had lost the ability to be an autonomous human being. My self-respect was tied to Wayne's level of respect for me. Everything I did for him was geared to raising his respect for me. I still did not understand that respect for oneself comes from within and is not dependent on external sources.

Friday 14th July

My eyes still weep but for Wayne it's all forgotten: he talked to me as if nothing happened last night. # On the way home, he started arguing again like he can't get enough of the drama and he yelled at me outside as we were about to go inside the house. Charmaine howled in fright because he was so loud then once inside the house he continued screaming, ranting that we had to divorce. We went to bed and we had a truce but he's been really touchy lately and yells at the slightest thing I say and nothing changes for the better. Even when we are talking it is an effort for me to respond and being nice to him despite his treatment of me makes me feel less of a person and more an extension of him. He

told me he resents me and blamed me # for the increased fighting.
  'Touchy lately'!!

Thursday 20th July

Wayne yelled at me for 'whingeing' about work and for 'letting my looks go' asking me if I was fat in the past because 'you have fat features and look like you were fat once'. How skinny does he want me to be? I'm only 7 stone 3 ounces now (and 5 feet 4 inches in height). Pam is still helping us with St Peter's. (She'd been threatening to quit working for us for weeks.) *During her work shift this afternoon, she and Heather* (another employee of ours) *had two drinks with Sister Margaret* (the then principal of St Peter's). *Pam must have had more drinks after that because she came back to the house after work, an hour late and she was slurring. We were there waiting for her to come home so that she could look after Charmaine while we finished the rest of the night's work. When we got back from work later she was in bed and according to Damian he'd hit Pam to stop her grabbing Charmaine off him.* (He wouldn't let Pam near Charmaine while she was drunk.) *So, she'd tried to ring the police and Barry had ripped the phone from the wall to prevent her doing so. Wayne dragged her out of the bedroom into the lounge room and screamed at her. Charmaine had been crying for an hour for me, Damian said, because of the fighting, and as soon as I picked her up she was quiet. It made me feel the best I have since she was born, knowing that she wanted her mother for the first time rather than Pam. We went home with me thinking what a family I'd married into and Wayne didn't improve matters when he argued with me once we were home.*

Sunday 13th August

I continually have to fend off Wayne's and Pam's belittling behaviour as well as contending with her obsession with Charmaine. She and Barry visited after lunch and she literally wrenched Charmaine from my arms. I hardly saw my daughter for the rest of the day and Pam wouldn't put her down or let me hold her. Charmaine loves her, laughs with her and didn't want to know me whenever I went near her to hold her for a change. Pam thinks Charmaine is hers and I'm getting more and more depressed and desperate whenever I think about the hold she has, and that Wayne encourages, over Charmaine. I was glad when they left at dark. Our wedding anniversary was today which we'd both forgotten until Pam reminded us and Wayne said: 'It means shit all to me.'

Wednesday 13th September

Wayne has been at me and at me all week calling me a joke and useless. Today while we were cleaning this huge mansion in Alka Springs with massive rooms and walls that had to be washed, Wayne turned to me and said: 'A man needs a woman, you look like a man all the time and I know heaps of women who go to work and still look good!' I was furious (we were cleaning filthy walls for God's sake and our line of work was hardly the same as working in an office.) After this job finished at 4pm, we cleaned St Peter's then the Civic Admin. from 5pm on and got home at about 11 when I then had to get dressed up for him and have sex.

Sunday 24th September

Wayne got drunk today and threw up and went to bed then

*screamed at me when Mum rang at 8pm, waking him. She'd
called to tell me Grandma had been rushed to hospital last night
in an ambulance with pains in her chest, the pain so intense she
was screaming from it. They took tests and found another blood
clot in her neck and Mum said she'd pay for a ticket for me to
come to the Gold Coast so I could see Grandma while she was
in hospital. Wayne said no to that: he didn't want me running
around up there and besides he couldn't spare me taking time off
from work (even though he tells me constantly that I'm a whinger
at work and not much use to him).*

Friday 17th November

Rick (my brother) *was visiting from the Gold Coast and he,
Wayne and I went out tonight to celebrate because I hadn't seen
him in ages and after we went downtown for a while, we ended
up at this friend of Wayne's place. I think the friend spiked my
drink because all of a sudden, I had to go outside and I was so sick
I fell down on the ground. Wayne came outside and screamed at
me for ruining his night out. He and Rick had to carry me back
to Pam's. Wayne was abusing me the whole time and Rick was
yelling at him for being such a pig for going on the way he was
about me being sick and messing his night up. Wayne put me to
bed on the blow-up bed in his parent's lounge room and when he
was undressing me he wanted sex and got really aggressive because
I was comatose and couldn't do anything.*

During our entire time, together, Wayne probably kissed
me passionately three times. He said kissing involved him
getting too close to another. I guess he meant both physically
and emotionally close. We averaged having sex three times a

week throughout our relationship at his insistence and every other night in between I masturbated him, myself wearing stockings. His demands that I wear not only stockings but high heels as well sickened me. Dressing up for him was mandatory; he would only have sex if I was 'accessorised'. If I hadn't dressed up, in the hope of avoiding sex, he would have used violence to achieve his ends, so I had no choice in the matter. This drove me to despair knowing that I couldn't refuse him and when he laid his hands on my stockinged legs my skin would crawl. Dressing up for him to have sex was particularly disturbing on Friday nights where a pattern had been established that involved performing for him while the football or cricket was being televised. The girls were made to go to bed before the sport's programs began, then without fail he would demand that I masturbated him or had intercourse in the lounge room regardless of how I felt. These activities were so entrenched that I would dread Friday night arriving and would dwell on it the entire week in between, to the extent that I could sense my physical body shutting down in response to my mental stress. I cannot now watch sports on television without reacting negatively. The sex was perfunctory, lacking affection; he was interested in me from the waist down only. I rarely said no to sex. The first time I denied him he verbally abused me for a week. The second time he physically abused me by punching me, dragging me off the lounge and ordering me to have sex with him. # The last time I said no caused his actions on the 5th of January 2003. At the edges of my consciousness I knew I was being violated yet I had to justify his actions by telling myself I should be grateful that he thought I was so irresistible he couldn't keep his hands off me. In the first few years of our relationship, this is what I told myself rather than face the truth of his continual use of control through sex (later I was no longer able to use this reasoning). That truth, of being violated, was horrible to contemplate; almost as bad as the sexual abuse itself, since to confront reality would mean having to leave, which was not an option (so I thought). At that time, I believed I was not strong enough to withstand the dire consequences which leaving him would incur. So, to keep myself safe and to maintain the status quo I shied away from examining his real motivations for wanting sex and continued to invent a fantasy land where we were a caring family unit.

1990

Monday 1st January

My brother Rick was at a crossroad in his life at this time and came to stay for an extended period on the property to rejuvenate and to revive our sibling relationship. However, he'd been at our house for only four days when, true to form, Wayne argued with Rick and me, ordering him to leave regardless of the fact that my brother had little money and was in a vulnerable frame of mind. The following day Wayne unceremoniously dumped Rick on the side of the highway heading north with only $30 on him and drove off. His actions alienated yet another member of my family. Wayne and I argued bitterly about Rick being made to leave but he wouldn't change his mind and said that he didn't want someone else in the house bludging off him. # He'd told me that I was disloyal to him for refusing to ask Rick to leave.

Whenever any of my family wanted or needed to stay with us, Wayne would argue with me for weeks against their visiting, until I became disillusioned and easily talked into believing that I was the selfish one for wanting them to stay.

Deborah Thomson

Sunday 21st January

Wayne continues to call me 'basically lazy'. He runs me down continually then pretends he loves me to keep me by his side # because no one else would put up with his behaviour and he knows it. I'm the idiot for staying.

Friday 9th March

Wayne tells me all the time that he'd prefer it if I drank more as he thinks he'd like me if I wasn't sober. My sobriety makes him think that in his words: 'We aren't right for each other.' What he means is that he thinks I'm boring if I'm not drinking every spare moment that we're at home, as he does.

Sunday 22nd April

Awful birthday as usual. I didn't even remember it was today then finally remembered halfway through work as Wayne hadn't mentioned it nor did he buy me a present. Worked from 9–4.30pm, went home and went to bed early and Charmaine almost choked vomiting in her sleep so I moved her into our bed to watch her and she vomited all night. Wayne was furious because she kept him awake.

Wednesday 25th April

I must have caught Charmaine's virus because I woke tonight with awful stomach cramps and stayed in the toilet for an hour vomiting which woke Wayne and he screamed at me, saying: 'Shut the fuck up, you're hacking like a 60-year-old and I can't get any sleep.' I feel so desperately alone and no matter how sick I am he'll make me go to work tomorrow.

Thursday 26th April

Still incredibly sick and I cried in the morning as Wayne didn't care less about how sick I was and I couldn't face the day but knew I had to go to work. I slept for an hour after the morning work then had the second shift and felt rotten all through it and had to drag myself through. Lay down for a moment before the night shift and tried to eat a pie for dinner after we got home and threw up again all night. Regardless of this Wayne wouldn't get up so I had to keep seeing to Charmaine as she was still off colour. Tonight, Wayne managed to sleep through everything so at least I didn't have him screaming at me as well.

Friday 27th April

Still sick all day and work was absolute murder, I had to keep running to the toilet to vomit. When we got home, Wayne watched the football on TV and I was so sick I fell asleep on the lounge room floor. I woke to Wayne shoving me with his foot to wake me because he wanted to go to bed.

Reading these entries may think I sound offhand or hardened to the abuse I was writing about. Nothing is further from the truth. While writing my diaries, I concentrated on the facts of the abuse rather than my emotional response to Wayne's violence. I found that I could not be emotional when writing. I had to be pragmatic because I was desperately trying to pretend ours was a normal relationship. I would not admit even to myself, in the pages of a diary that the abuse was affecting me emotionally. If I had really examined the devastating effect of Wayne's actions I might have concluded that it was time to leave and I was not prepared to take such a drastic measure, yet.

Deborah Thomson

Thursday 17th May

Wayne screamed at me so much today that I told him that the only reason I couldn't leave him was because I'd lose Charmaine and he said: 'That's not the only thing you'd lose. Try leaving and I'll shoot you like a dog and don't think I won't.' The look in his eyes made me think that he really would kill me if I tried to take Charmaine and leave.

Wednesday 4th July

He only loves a person if they act the way he wants them to. # He hates Charmaine when she cries and he hates me when I'm depressed and he screams at both of us whenever these occur.

Tuesday 7th August

Wayne woke up in a filthy mood yelled at bubs (Charmaine) for waking him up then screamed at me for accidentally taking the blankets off him in bed during the night so I got off the bed and I cried from anger and hatred toward him and he said: 'You're a whinger, always whinging, and I'm sick of you.'

Sunday 12th August

He remembered our anniversary and made me get dressed up when we got home from work and we had sex with Charmaine in the bed as well and he wouldn't leave me alone even though I tried to put Charmaine in her bed. He got really angry and said that he couldn't wait for me to put her to bed and if I didn't give it to him right then I'd be sorry. He didn't care at all that she was in bed with us.

Thursday 23rd August

*Wayne is so sarcastic and picky about what I say, do and wear #
that I am crying every day and have a rotten headache most days.
It's a nightmare getting through each day. I'm getting desperate
and losing hope that I can keep handling this life.*

Tuesday 2nd October

*I forgot to bring the account for the Civic Admin. to town to hand
in so Wayne as usual screamed at me all night at work. I didn't
talk to him when we got home. I told him he upset me and he
said: 'I don't care,' and laughed at me because he really doesn't
care, I'm just 'another bitch he's going out with.' Later he was all
over me because he wanted sex, I can't stand him near me.*

Monday 26th November

*Wayne as usual doesn't speak to me when we're out and doesn't
speak to me at home except to scream or sulk in a bad mood
like he's doing today. He's only in a bad mood with me, talks
to everyone else. # I literally have nobody to talk to except his
mother who is annoyed with me most of the time; she blames me
for Wayne's bad moods and says I should work harder so that
he's not so tired from working hard. She says I'm not pulling my
weight otherwise Wayne wouldn't be so tired and cranky.*

Saturday 15th December

Mum and Grandma came for three days over Christmas. (That's
as long as Wayne would 'allow' them to stay in the house.)
*We all went to bed early as there was nothing on TV. Wayne and
Grandma talked to each other. However, Mum and Wayne didn't*

speak to each other unless through necessity. Grandma later told Mum that she only speaks to the 'animal' because she is trying to keep the peace. She's scared of him when he drinks as he has a temper and dislikes him because she can't work him out. Wayne won't let me visit them at the Gold Coast so they have to come to me if we are to see each other and then it is only for three days and cannot be on Christmas Day, has to be before or after as Wayne insists he and I spend Christmas Day with only his family. Every time they leave knowing that it'll be a year at least before they can come back here I cry and am so unhappy it takes days before I can control my sadness.

I was finally beginning to realise just how toxic our relationship was and had always been, however too much was invested in our remaining together [I thought]. My stubborn belief that Wayne would change and that his changing would somehow mitigate everything he'd done to my family and me, kept me in a fool's paradise and provided fertile ground for the abuse to flourish.

1991

Tuesday 1st January

We had a day off from work. Wayne was really friendly and talkative and upbeat and we got along for once. I will try to be more affectionate and dress in a more feminine way and maybe we can be like this more often. # It was a good day.

Thursday 10th January

During a break from work Wayne went downtown and bought two pairs of stockings for me and a bottle of Bourbon. I'm worth that much when he wants sex, it's a good day when I do what I'm told.

Monday 14th January

The hiatus didn't last long. # On the way home from work today Wayne was angry for no reason I could think of and he turned on me in the car and started screaming at me, saying he hated me and he was sick of everything. When we got home he went straight to bed which was good because I didn't want to look at him.

Tuesday 15th January

Wayne is back to fighting badly with me and when he isn't yelling we are just wary around each other and I keep out of his way.

Friday 18th January

Wayne and Pam had another huge fight over her not working in place of Heather (they were both employees for us at this time) and they screamed at each other in front of Charmaine. We drove home and he screamed at me, again in front of Charmaine. All she hears is everyone around her screaming. Pam knows how to stir Wayne up then he takes it out on me because his mother can never be at fault, so it must be my fault. #

Wayne's relationship with his mother was problematic. He wanted and continually attempted to gain his mother's unconditional love and approval acquiescing to every demand she made on him. Daily she demanded that he give her less work within the business, increase her babysitting for Charmaine and rid himself of the albatross around his neck (his wife). Unfortunately, these same demands would slightly differ from day to day: more work and less babysitting then less work and more babysitting the following day (always the same demand where I was concerned, her other about-faces were crazy-making) so that it didn't matter what Wayne did for Pam, it was never enough and not to her liking. His gaining her love seemed to be an impossibility. However, Wayne could not accept that his mother was less than perfect. Pam had to remain on the pedestal at all costs therefore if she was disillusioned or unhappy the cause of her discontent came from outside of herself, Wayne reasoned. Pam blamed me for Wayne's discontent, Wayne blamed me for Pam's discontent; I was the perfect scapegoat.

Thursday 24th January

Wayne is either in a hurry to get the sex done or he is rough and gets cranky if I don't get rough too. Tonight, he was so rough his shoulder bones and fingers dug into my skin, hard. I could hardly breathe and panicked wanting to get it over with because I thought I was suffocating and his fingers were hurting me, digging into my arms.

Sunday 3rd February

Wayne and I dropped in to the Grand after work last night to see Steve and today Wayne went on and on about how Steve really liked me and also Greg (friend of Wayne's who was there last night too) *did as well and that he was jealous and didn't want to take me out again, too much of a hassle when he had to 'fight guys off all night'. # I thought about how much Wayne tells me that I've had it, I'm getting old looking, I dress like a dag etcetera so how come he's worried about other men if I'm so ugly?*

Tuesday 12th February

Perry (friend of Wayne's who lived on a property in Interim, a small community on the way home to our place) *and Wayne got drunk at his place then we drove home and the whole time we were there at Perry's my ribs hurt. They are sore, only bruised I hope from falling on the edge of Charmaine's cot the other night when Wayne came in and pushed me in anger, while I was putting her to bed. Didn't get any sleep last night as they are so painful and I couldn't use my right hand today at work as it pulls my ribs when I stretch my arm.* (Years later, I had my ribs x-rayed and two ribs showed signs of past fractures.)

Deborah Thomson

Saturday 16th February

Wayne wanted to stop in at the 'top pub' in Urindy after work so we did and conversation was stilted until a friend of Wayne's came over. Wayne drank a lot of beer and he drove home drunk and of course we had a fight about me earning my keep for the rest of my life or I'd be 'no use to him'. I went out on the verandah and sat with a rotten headache but Wayne made up later so I would have sex with him then we went to bed. I had a migraine by then.

Sunday 24th March

At the Bus Terminal (one of our cleaning contracts) we cleaned the windows and Wayne and I fought all the way through them then went inside to clean. Wayne was yelling at me to shut up about something I'd said and the manager, Jan, walked in unexpectedly, heard him and was really strange around us until she left. Later Wayne was angry for being caught abusing me and said he was taking Charmaine home and 'You're not coming; this is the finish.' I said 'fine with me' but we can never be finished, I'd die if Charmaine was taken away. We fought all afternoon once we got home too. (Yes, I went home with him despite my protestations.) ★

Tuesday 2nd April

I had a feeling I was pregnant and we weren't even trying (neither of us wanted any more children) so I had a blood test today and I was pregnant, had been for only two weeks, yet I knew. I am worried about bringing another child into this environment but am going to have it. Having an abortion is not an option.

Thursday 4th April

I have a funny feeling about this baby, can't shake the feeling that something is wrong and when I told Wayne he said: 'It might be sick. Don't count on it too much.' We went to work and cleaned a filthy house in Warburg. It took three hours, then we got back to Alka Springs at 1pm, had lunch, cleaned a house in Glass Street and mowed the lawn then St Peter's, had a break for dinner then did the night run finished at 9.30pm, got home at 10.30. I feel so tired, not like when I was carrying Charmaine and that worries me.

Saturday 6th April

Hamish (friend of Wayne's and building our house on the property) *came out early to do some building. I rang Dad to tell him I was pregnant then after lunch I started bleeding so I lay down. Hamish said he could take me in his car to hospital but Wayne said no I'd be fine so I just went to bed early feeling so tired.*

Tuesday 9th April

Went to Dr Marlboro as I'm still bleeding heavily and he said the baby is still there in the womb and seems to be okay so it was best for me to rest. Wayne had to help me do the shopping because I felt so weak. It is awful being like this.

Wednesday 10th April

Went with Pam, Toby (an employee) *and Wayne and cleaned the Glass Street house (so much for resting) and I had severe cramps like period pains and it felt more painful than labour. Bled heavier than ever at work so I had to see Dr Marlboro that afternoon and he said the baby is still inside me but has dropped in the womb. I went back to work and just couldn't stand up the cramps were so bad, but I had to keep working or everyone would have come down on me and told me how lazy I was.*

Thursday 11th April

I did the art museum, cleaned the Butler Lane unit, then the Civic Admin. tonight. After that, I had to hose out the Bus Terminal following cleaning of the gas company building. I was in terrible pain all through, could hardly walk, shouldn't have gone at all except Wayne had to travel to Sydney tonight (he visited a friend for a few days) *and he was busting to get out the door.*

Friday 12th April

I saw Dr Marlboro at 11am and had to go into hospital at 2pm. I miscarried and saw the embryo—it was about three inches long. I was shocked. I was anesthetised for a curette then later went back to Pam's to stay while Wayne was away.

Saturday 13th April

Damian, Pam and I did the weekend work. It took us four hours between us. I felt faint after and everyone said I looked pale and sick. Wayne got back at 2am from Sydney and I pretended to be asleep. He said later that he looked in on Charmaine and me and kissed us on the forehead but I knew that he'd really just walked straight down the hallway without even coming into the room. He just dove into his own bed.

Sunday 14th April

I felt so depressed and Wayne didn't give me any sign of sympathy. We went to work early in the morning to get it done and I cried in the car on the way home to our place. I am so tired during work at the moment.

Monday 15th April

Cleaned the art museum then did the shopping then had the night run. I'm bleeding again and have had a terrible headache behind the eyes and the temples since yesterday and have had to take Mersyndol all day to try and get rid of it but nothing helps. I feel so depressed and helpless and hopeless right now to the point of desperation. I masturbated Wayne tonight when we got home because he hadn't let up the entire day about me being a burden so I felt that I had to prove my value.

Monday 22nd April

Did the art museum then shopping, Wayne didn't remember my birthday until after Pam had told him when we got to town this morning. He didn't say anything. We just had a beer at lunchtime before the night run but didn't do anything special today. Some thirtieth!

Thursday 25th April

Had sex tonight, the first since the miscarriage. Wayne couldn't wait any longer.

Tuesday 7th May

Didn't have to go to work until 2.30pm so Wayne had sex with me on the lounge room floor whether I wanted to or not, then we did it again tonight after work.

Friday 24th May

Wayne slipped on cat food by the front door tonight and came in screaming that I was a cunt for leaving it there and if I didn't say sorry there'd be trouble. When I didn't apologise, he went to bed three quarters of the way through his beloved football on TV. I thought, he could scream about a bit of cat food, yet I went to work during and straight after a miscarriage with hardly a murmur about how awful I felt.

Saturday 15th June

Wayne has been fighting all day with me so much that I am feeling suicidal. I really am sick of it all and Charmaine is the only thing here that keeps me from dropping my bundle.

Wednesday 19th June

Same as usual work day except that it's Wayne's birthday so I had to get dressed up (always stockings, high heels and a tight dress) when we arrived home tonight and have sex. With Wayne, it feels like I'm going through the motions, he doesn't seem to be aware of me at all and I'm certainly not of him. Having forced intimacy every other night regardless of how tired or sick I am with colds or migraines and being expected to dress up like he's taking me out for dinner when I'm really just getting home from work, has me so depressed and sick at heart that I haven't really tried to analyse how deeply wounding this routine is.

I was afraid to examine the true horror of it because I

sensed that the sexual abuse was quite possibly more injurious to my sanity than the physical and emotional abuse, due to the extended close proximity to Wayne that the act entailed. Throughout our relationship, as well as not kissing me, he didn't hug me or show any of the gestures of affection; for instance, hand on the back, stroking of hair or cheek, hand holding in public, that I now know is part of a healthy and loving relationship. Because of this lack the sexual act reeked of hollowness. The necessity of being naked, often confronting at any time for people before sex, and having to be physically close to Wayne, was abhorrent to me. Yet I had no choice but to be intimate with him. As mentioned earlier, the once or twice I had previously said no resulted in painful consequences that I didn't want to risk being repeated. It is doubly shocking that not only did I not receive affection from Wayne, I also didn't expect such gestures from him, thinking that I didn't deserve these normal signs of love. I was content just to have a day where he wasn't screaming at me. That to me was his way of displaying affection. Having a demonstrably affectionate man in my life now, I feel nauseated when I recall the years wasted waiting and hoping for Wayne to be other than he was.

Tuesday 25th June

Wayne is so arrogant and aggressive toward me and he's completely different when he's with everyone else, he raves on to them and hardly talks to me. # Yet, I'm expected to work then go home and never have any of my friends out here while Wayne has mates out every other weekend. I have to be with him only, can't talk to anyone else or I get into trouble. #

Deborah Thomson

Friday 19th July

Mum rang and Wayne was in the kitchen listening. Apparently, I didn't say the right things to her, he thought I was criticising him to her. He came up behind me as I was putting the phone down and grabbed my neck and half-choked me from behind. He left red marks on my neck and my throat half closed as he was lifting me off the ground by my neck. I tried to hit him off me so he went to hit me and he said: 'I hate you. I really do.' We went to work and later he said: 'Everyone gets sick of each other and fights after they've been married a long time.' !! # Watched football after we got home then went to bed and had sex.

Thursday 25th July

Cleaned the Ryan Street house then had a huge artwork dusting job at the art museum then did some business downtown then the night run, all the time Wayne fighting with me. I am so sick of all this work and anger. My body feels like it's dying on me.

Sunday 28th July

Tooth started aching last night and kept aching all through the work today at Gum leaves preschool, Gas Building window cleaning and the Civic Admin. Hamish came out with Fiona (his wife) to our home in the afternoon and they went off to get firewood down the road. When they got back Wayne thought I'd said something rude to Fiona and screamed at me after they left for being rude to her. I woke at 11.30pm in agony with the tooth and stayed awake for the rest of the night popping painkillers which gave me no relief and Wayne yelled at me for crying and waking him up. He didn't care that I was in so much pain. I slept on the lounge to get away from his whinging. Got up at 3.30am again, we had to get up at 3.45 anyway for work.

Monday 29th July

Wayne and I fought all day, he is giving me no support, just sick of my whinging, he says. I hated his insensitivity and Pam didn't help, saying that she wouldn't go to work for me so that I could rest. I took Mersyndol on the hour while we did the art museum then the shopping and I was in that much pain I couldn't think straight so finally went to the dentist at 12.30pm, had an extraction, then back to work. I was in so much pain after the numbness wore off I was doubling over with it. Will this never end?

Friday 9th August

I can't believe it but I feel pregnant.

Monday 12th August

Cleaned the art museum then went shopping then tried the pregnancy test at 2.30pm and it was positive and I was worried about saying anything after the last scare then told Wayne, and he was excited as he thinks it will be a boy and wants to call it Shamus and he refused to let me have any say about the baby's name. He'd named Charmaine as well and I had no choice. The same as everything Wayne wants; he always gets his own way. (This is all I worried about at the time? Who had naming rights?) *I seem to fall pregnant easily and want to bring this one up differently with far less input from Pam.*

Deborah Thomson

Monday 2nd September

I have been vomiting and really sick on and off for weeks and thinking that I might lose this baby when I have to work all day whether I'm sick or not. It's not as if we don't have others who can do the work. When Wayne went to Sydney, his mother happily filled in for him but when I'm so sick I can hardly stand, no one wants to fill in for me. Instead I have Wayne and Pam fighting with me and her telling him how lazy I am. I can't see Dr Marlboro until the 19th. Went shopping after I picked up the referral to the doctor then had the afternoon and night work. Wayne cleaned the bus terminal windows and let me stay at home while he did that.

Thursday 12th September

Wayne and I aren't getting along at all. At work this morning he yelled at me and told me I was a pig and to shut up. So now we aren't talking. I cried all morning and things were tense. Why don't I leave?

Friday 4th October

Clive, the builder, delivered the red cedar planks for the lounge room and family room walls early in the morning. Wayne went back to bed after they left, thank goodness, because I didn't want to talk to him after last night when he'd hit me in the eye with his pillow, trying to hit Charmaine with it. She'd been crying from being sick and had woken us. He was in a filthy mood the rest of the day when he did get up.

Sunday 10th November

Wayne has been going out at night a lot lately and we stay in town at his parents when he goes out. Every time he comes back around 3am and wakes me to tell me about some 'gorgeous chick' who would love to go out with him. Last night it was Dianna's (friend of Wayne's) sister who was 'after him all night' and that 'she had it all.' I just wish he'd stop talking about these women because he'll never leave me for anyone else. No one else would put up with him. No wonder his mother was so keen to keep us together.

I knew at that time that no one would live with Wayne so why on earth did I continue to do that! The dichotomy that no one else would have Wayne and yet I must do everything to keep him interested in me so that he wouldn't feel the need to look for someone else, shows how skewed and counter-productive my reasoning was. And thus, how unlikely it was that I could think logically enough to formulate a decent plan to leave him.

Wednesday 27th November

Wayne screamed at me worse than he usually does and fought with me all day on the way to work, at work and until we went to bed. I dreaded having to go home with him when we live so far out of town with no neighbours near to hear us should anything bad happen.

Thursday 28th November

Went downtown after the art museum to pay bills then fought with Wayne at his parents' home because I'd lost a cheque payment from work somewhere. He continued fighting with me all through work. When we got home I had sex with him when he 'asked' because I was desperate to calm him down. This is the only means left to stop him yelling at me.

Although Wayne hadn't been particularly physically violent towards me for a while we didn't go one day for months at a time without him screaming at me, denigrating me and isolating me from my friends, none of whom I'd seen since Narene fell out with me in July 1986. I literally didn't have one friend I could confide in. Only Wayne's friends came out to the property and I was expected to play host to them without of course acting too friendly, in case Wayne thought I was flirting. The only person I remotely had to converse with was his mother. I was allowed to talk to her because she sided with him in every argument therefore didn't present a threat to his control over me.

*Wayne at first would play on my feelings of guilt to stop me leaving him; somehow, he knew that I felt responsible for every fight between us. As the relationship progressed I became more and more invested in staying due to marriage, having a daughter, a property and a business. He turned to behaviour which threatened my losing all these things of which I had worked hard for and valued, should I try to leave. His threats were, as he often said, 'to keep me in my place.' His threats of violence against me, the death threats and the worst threat of all for me, taking Charmaine away and letting his mother rear her prevented me from seriously considering leaving though I often said I would in the heat of the moment. I instinctively knew that my survival would be in question should any actual attempt be made to remove myself and Charmaine from the home, resulting in her being cared for by Pam, were I to die. Pam's parenting of Wayne, I knew, was partly the cause of his violent behaviour towards women and therefore the idea of her raising Charmaine was not to be entertained.

1992

Wayne found this year's diary and destroyed it. I have an excellent memory and can recall episodes that occurred although not the actual day or month they occurred in. Apart from the more violent episodes, life carried on much as before, working continuously even in the last trimester of pregnancy, unwarranted yelling and screaming on Wayne's part and the inevitable sex every two to three days.

Tuesday 7th April

Louise (again Wayne chose the name) was born after a six-hour labour at approximately 9pm weighing 7lbs 13 ounces. It was a difficult birth with Louise stressing so much during the labour that she was close to death when the doctor finally arrived and pulled her from my body. I was determined to bring this daughter up in my own home without relying on Pam who would I knew would try to turn her against me as Charmaine had been turned against me. In arguing to stay at home more, I stood my ground for the first time in years. I refused to go to work every day; rather, I would remain at home on the property three days a week to bond with my baby. I had to endure flak from both Wayne and Pam for months over my decision. Indeed, I believe that Pam thought, until the end of our relationship, that I had harmed Wayne beyond repair by absenting myself from the daily business work. Unfortunately, my hard-won resolve didn't achieve much else aside from my spending more time with my second daughter than I had with the first. In a matter of months Pam refused to do the work I had done previously so I had to return to work. My being at home meant that Pam did not care for Charmaine on a daily basis and she sorely resented me for having the chance to raise the girls rather than doing that herself.

June

Wayne was in the kitchen screaming at me. I was in the lounge room. Suddenly he appeared by my side and pushed me to the ground and kicked me twice in the side. He was wearing his steel-capped work boots. I couldn't breathe and he sneered and said that he knew how and where to hit me so that bruises wouldn't show. He knew, he said, because he'd been thrown in jail overnight and had seen how the police hit a man all over with telephone books: 'Maximum pain without the evidence of a beating,' he said. He told me that if I didn't wake up to myself he'd do the same to me. Following this violence, he threatened to shoot me if I were to tell anyone about his kicking me.

Later that day he dismissed the threat, saying I should understand that it was empty, knowing as I did 'how much he loved and couldn't live without me'. # Dismissals such as this or outright denial of an incident, used to confuse me almost to the point of insanity. His diminishing or denial of abuse, which he may have thought mitigated the act, felt (as mentioned earlier) for me like I'd been doubly abused, with twice the negative effects on my psyche. I would then begin to wonder whether I'd misunderstood his meaning or even whether I had heard him say it at all, and this last thought caused me to doubt my sanity. My grip on reality would slip to the extent where I became a fractured, disturbed human being, unable to discern truth from fiction, despite knowing deeply that his behaviour was hurtful and unwarranted.

July

Wayne grabbed my left arm and squeezed it so hard bruises came up from his fingers by the time we got to town. Because he was in a bad mood when we arrived in town, Pam became annoyed with me for as she immediately assumed, not looking after Wayne properly. I mustn't have been looking after him, she said, because he was so tired and cranky lately. Listening to her run me down upset me so I said: 'You don't know what I go through living with Wayne,' and showed her the bruises. She just looked at me and said I must have done something to deserve getting the bruises and they were 'nothing'; Barry had pointed a gun at her once when he and she were arguing. As Pam said this I knew that she was not what I had stupidly hoped deep down she might have been: a last bastion of defence against Wayne's abuse. Finally, I understood that I was truly alone in this nightmare. I never again sought her advice or assistance in matters of abuse.

Deborah Thomson

August

Wayne was arguing with me in our bedroom when suddenly without warning he raised his fist to punch me in the head, hit out at me and punched a hole in the cupboard instead. His fist went through the plywood cupboard door and he sneered: 'That should have been your face.' Whether his intention had been to hit me and hitting the cupboard was accidental I do not know. I suspect the former was his intention as the cupboards were a present to him from his grandmother so he would not have intentionally wanted to damage them. Had his fist connected with my head it would have caused much damage as it took quite a lot of force to break through the cupboard door the way it had.

October

We drove into Wayne's parent's front yard on our way to work and Wayne began to yell at me while parking the car. I jumped out of the passenger's side but inadvertently hooked my sleeve into the car door handle. Wayne was still yelling when he noticed my struggle to free myself from the handle. He immediately took off and I found myself running alongside the car feeling at any moment that I would be dragged underneath. I screamed at him to stop, the noise alerting the neighbour who ran outside to determine the cause of the screaming. Wayne on seeing the man turned off the motor and pretended to be concerned about my being caught on the handle. I went inside his parent's home shaking and upset but said nothing to them.

1993

I don't include as many entries unless they contain violence of a different nature to that described previously.

Thursday 18th February

Wayne and I fought all day over Louise crying last night and waking him. He delighted in using last night's event as evidence of my uselessness as a mother and how sure he was that his mother would have 'sorted Louise out'. I am depressed because none of my family is here who will take me as I am, not denigrate me but support me when my child cries. I have to be someone else all the time here when the only people I have contact with hate me. I can't talk to anyone; they are outsiders, not like a real family who accept you for who you are.

Saturday 27th February

Wayne and I had an awful fight and he picked Charmaine up and threw her over his shoulder still hanging onto her arm and he nearly broke it. He said later he didn't know why he did that to her and wouldn't again but I'd better stop messing with his head he said because 'I (Wayne) get out of control and I don't know what I'll do next.'

Deborah Thomson

Wednesday 3rd March

I'm sick of hearing from Pam that Wayne works harder than me and from Wayne that I don't 'pull my weight' and that he 'won't forget it'. What do I have to do to prove myself and why should I have to? I'm becoming so desperate to change things for good. I wish he'd find another woman; only she'd have to work like a dog, treat him like a king and get kicked in return.

Friday 26th March

When we got home from work and were driving up to the front gate I was too scared to open it because there were huge moths everywhere, in plague proportions and I hated them so much I didn't care that he was screaming at me to get out and open the gate. (I have an intense phobia of moths stemming from early childhood and break out in a sweat and shake whenever one is near me.) *That night there were thousands flying in the car headlights, and I cowered on the front seat like a whipped dog. He kept screaming and pushing me but I would not move so he got out, slammed the car door and opened the gate. God did he go on, slamming doors and revving the car and kangaroo-hopping the vehicle right up the driveway to the front door. More moths were there and I would have happily slept in the car for the night but he dragged me out of the car and pushed me roughly into the house. He called me a self-centred whore for not opening the gate.*

Sunday 18th April

Wayne said I disgusted him because I couldn't stop Louise crying in the middle of the night and that I was a lousy mother. The usual refrain but hearing him say it hurts every time.

Thursday 22nd April

Worked all day; the art museum then extra windows to clean which took an hour and a half longer, then downtown for some business stuff, then the usual horrible night run. Some lousy birthday, no one wished me happy birthday. Wayne didn't even offer to buy me a drink to celebrate. Instead he went out to Bob's for two and a half hours after work, leaving the girls and I with Pam.

Friday 7th May

Another nightmare day: Wayne fought with me and at one point grabbed my collar and shook me repeatedly. He came back to his parents at 6pm after St Peter's to get me for the night cleaning run and I was really sick, probably brought on by the earlier fight and Wayne was really angry and screamed, then we went to work and neither of us talked for the rest of the night. It's frightening how sarcastic he is to me, almost constantly. If it weren't for the kids, I'd do us both a favour and leave him.

Wednesday 9th June

Have been trying to keep away from Wayne, he is in such a bad mood, says I get everything I want while he's out working for it. Sure.

Friday 6th August

It's a wonder I don't have mood swings since life here is unbearable with the same things happening day after day and absolutely no one to talk to. Wayne doesn't know what it's like never to have family around. Had to clean St Peter's chapel and Pam, as usual, was trying to run our lives, told Barry to look after the kids next Friday so I could go to work as she thinks it's too much for Wayne without me. Whenever we go to town she tells me what to do about work or how to bring up the kids or she's telling Wayne I have to work more. She can't stand the thought of me not slaving. Damian and Deidre (Wayne's sister-in-law now married to Damian) have the sense to live separate lives away from her influence. Wayne is still very much tied to her apron strings. The way he lets her dictate to him is obscene. I can't voice my opinion about anything and I feel like I'm losing both kids to her the longer she looks after them. Wayne and her made me return to work fulltime because she wouldn't do the work. I had to come back to replace her and I feel like I don't exist except to be the brunt of everyone's anger or a slave to their inconsistent demands. As well, the kids treat me like I'm not worth much because they listen to Pam and Wayne criticise me for everything wrong in their own lives. I want to hit my head against the wall repeatedly just to get these wretched, desperate thoughts of what my life has disintegrated to, out.

Sunday 22nd August

We had a hell of a fight this morning and Wayne carried it on through work then into the night after we got home. I put Louise in Charmaine's room to sleep so I could sleep in Louise's room because I couldn't stop crying. Wayne came in and punched my arm, told me to shut up then dragged me back to our bedroom and still I cried as I thought about how my life had degenerated to this where all I do every second is walk around tensed for the next screaming episode. Wayne's screaming mostly comes from out of the blue, no rhyme or reason for it # and this makes me even tenser.

Monday 30th August

After a week of the worst fights, Wayne said to me this morning: 'If you didn't look like a hag all of the time I'd go to bed with you more.' !! Then he quickly said: 'No really, you're beautiful and I'd love you all my life even if you left.' I just felt sick and said: 'I have to go, this isn't working,' and straightaway he said I could go but there's no way the kids were going with me.

Readers may wonder why I continued to take notice of his repeated threat regarding the girls, however due to the threat being screamed at me and often accompanied by pushing and shoving or moves towards the bedroom where the guns were stored I always took his words and actions seriously each time they occurred. The more the noise and chaos within the house the more I strove to do whatever I thought necessary to negate the stress and that included taking his threat as gospel, threats that were an obvious outcome of my inability to be a good wife so I thought.

Saturday 4th September

Had to get dressed up for Wayne then we had sex in Louise's bed 'for something different' he said, then he dragged me into our bedroom and we had sex again. Later he made me have sex when we went to bed to sleep. He continually issues ultimatums like: 'Dress up or I'll find another woman and she'll bring the kids up. You'll never see them again,' or 'I liked you better when you didn't have the kids. You should drink more and maybe you'd be interesting.' He wants his image of me, not who I really am, so I'll never really love him and the decent thing would be to leave but I don't know how to do that when there is no outside support at all.

Saturday 11th September

Had a huge fight in the bedroom before we had sex. He said he'd have to bash his way out of this argument and he pushed and shoved me around the bedroom repeatedly, putting his hands on my shoulders and shoving me backwards and I wasn't just scared but also almost blacking out from fury at how he was treating me. Then he deliberately this time, bashed another hole in the clothes cupboard door and said: 'That'll be your head next,' and I became really scared and tried to run out of the room. He grabbed me and threw me on the bed and said that I wasn't going anywhere and there was no one to stop him, he could do what he liked. He wouldn't let me out of the bedroom for an hour, just kept throwing me back on the bed whenever I tried to leave the room and the kids were crying and calling out for me. Eventually he got tired of it all and went to bed.

Thursday 28th October

I forgot to take the list of what lights we needed to buy for home before the electrician came out to install them, so couldn't go down town to buy them and Wayne did his nut, screamed at me and called me an incompetent cunt and what little work I did was a 'pimple on his backside'. I screamed back at him from sheer frustration and desperation at having to endure his screaming at me over nothing, yet again. Lately I've noticed that I constantly have tension headaches and taking Panadol at least twice a day to get rid of the pain.

Sunday 7th November

The entire family went to see Slim Dusty at Green Valley Farm on the way to Idyll town. Wayne got really drunk and belligerent at the concert then when we got home he wanted sex and said that he wanted me to hurt him during it. He wanted me to be aggressive and to take charge and he wanted me to kick and punch him. I said: 'You're disgusting,' and wouldn't, but I think he was too drunk to notice that I was refusing him and thankfully, he fell asleep. I couldn't sleep for a long time as I reflected on the implications of what he'd wanted sexually. I hope that he doesn't have any memory of this when he wakes up tomorrow.

Wednesday 1st December

Wayne has been teaching me to drive a manual car all week and screams so much and calls me hopeless and the worst driver he's ever seen every time he takes me out, that I become the worst driver ever. I'm sure he's making it so hard for me to learn so that I can't drive on my own and have some freedom. Today when he was teaching me he got angry at me stalling the car at the intersection, punched my left arm so hard I couldn't lift it up to the steering wheel and had to let him drive.

Thursday 2nd December

Wayne was so angry this morning he lost control at the art museum, out in public which he normally doesn't do. He grabbed my chin and shook my head then shoved me into the front glass door of the building so that the door rattled. He made up later saying I should be more patient with him # and he'd try not to be so angry.

Deborah Thomson

Wednesday 8th December

Within two minutes of being in each other's company Wayne is snapping or yelling at me then tonight he grabbed me in the bedroom and wanted sex so I performed my duty and must have been unresponsive enough for even him to notice because he laughed sarcastically and said: 'Where's the romance? I'll start thinking you don't love me anymore,' and he laughed again.

Friday 10th December

We had a hell of a fight today. Wayne slapped my face for crying and I told him he made me feel like dirt and he said he didn't know why I should feel that way because he loved me. I screamed 'like crap you do' I was so sickened to hear him say that, and he screamed at me and called me useless and stupid. We had to calm down to go to work, then I masturbated him when we got back home. To touch him makes me feel so sick it would almost be worth the consequences if I said no.

Tuesday 21st December

Mum and Grandma were down for Christmas and poor Mum has to put up with being in the same room with Wayne when they can't stand each other. Bad day today, great holiday my family are having, it's the visit from hell. Mum, Louise and I were in the kitchen when the phone rang and it was Sister Margaret from St Peter's calling to speak to Wayne. He was on the phone talking to her when Louise fell off her highchair hitting her chin on the tiles. Mum yelled out 'oh shit' instinctively, she was so worried, and Sister Margaret heard it over the phone. When Wayne finished the call, I knew he wasn't worried about Louise, didn't even look at her to see if she was injured, instead he screamed at Mum for embarrassing him in front of his boss. Mum said: 'How can you not worry about a little girl who's just hit her head on the hard floor?' Wayne kept screaming at Mum so her and Grandma packed their clothes and stayed at Tatts for the night before getting the bus back to the Gold Coast the next day, rather than spend another night under Wayne's roof.

This year's theme of belittling me, denouncing my parenting skills, reducing me to a sexual object, a human devoid of personality and not deserving of even the basic rights repelled me but also had the deleterious effect of making me more reliant on Wayne as the source of my happiness. As my sense of autonomy diminished so I became more enmeshed in keeping him happy. Wayne had taught me to suppress my needs and supplant my rights with his needs.

1994

Saturday 8th January

We'd been at Wayne's cousin Katrina's wedding and went back to his parents in a taxi at midnight. As soon as we got out of the taxi, Wayne said he 'wanted it' in the Jackaroo (our car was parked in his parent's front yard for the night). He said: 'Say no if you like,' so I did and he exploded, called me a whore and that 'I wasn't worth a pinch of shit' and so on, and even after his tirade he wanted me to take his boots off when we got inside! I told him to go and get another woman to take his boots off, so he said: 'I'll just do that, you're no fucking good to me,' and took off in our car drunk. Pam got up and we stayed awake until 4am and he still hadn't returned. All Pam could worry about was whether he might crash.

Sunday 9th January

Wayne had apparently driven back to our place last night. He arrived back later today at his parents and took myself and the kids home. I dreaded going back there and my fears were well-founded as Wayne let off a litany of screaming that lasted all afternoon and I had to go to bed early and pretend I was asleep to escape.

Deborah Thomson

Tuesday 11th January

Wayne calls my attempts to discuss issues 'nagging'. So, on the way to town, when I was talking about his words and actions the previous Saturday and trying to reason with him, (when will I learn to keep my thoughts to myself?) while he was driving, with the kids in the backseat and myself in the front, he suddenly let go of the wheel and threw me against the passenger door. My head hit the window hard and dazed me then he pulled my hair and yanked my head down onto the seat so hard my neck cracked and I almost blacked out with the pain. He kept punching me in the right arm until it bruised while repeatedly grabbing my face and squeezing it. I had to hit his arm twice before he'd let go of my face and I cried that all of his other girlfriends left him before they got a chance to nag him. He slammed the brakes on, stopped the car, opened my door and shoved me then got out and dragged me out of the car and took off. I was shaking and so adrenalin-filled that I felt faint and just stood there in shock and shivering, wondering what had just happened. A few minutes later he came back, got out of the car and hugged me and tried to apologise and put me back in the front seat, the kids crying hysterically by now. We drove to his parents' place to drop the kids off and went inside for a coffee before work. I went straight into the spare bedroom without saying hello to anyone and I heard Pam say to Wayne: 'What's wrong with her?' Neither Wayne nor the kids said anything about the incident so his parents never did find out about it. Pam just assumed I was being moody. While he was hitting me in the car, he was screaming that I could piss off, he would keep the kids because I was insane and I could never look after them. He also said: 'Try and take them and you'll find out what I'm really capable of.' I called him a mad man.

I took his threats seriously and would do anything to avoid finding out just what he was 'capable of' because I was [and still am] of a very slight build, physically incapable of taking the children from him without serious injury to myself, had physical retribution come to fruition as threatened. During our relationship, I had never been able to stand up to him in physical combat. Readers may wonder why I stood up for myself at all during such violent altercations, but I occasionally did because I believed that *he was a rational man despite his violence* therefore we could argue or debate as normal couples did without resorting to abuse. I still could not conceive that he wasn't hitting me because I'd somehow deserved such treatment! Such thoughts indicated a deep-seated misconception of my self-worth and allowed him, probably encouraged him in his own reasoning, to lash out at me because he too thought that I'd brought on his abuse. Actually, the word abuse was not in his vocabulary. In his mind, *I was causing* him to act in what he believed to be perfectly natural responses to 'back chat, a rebellious streak' on my part that shouldn't be tolerated by him. Therefore, I deserved to be reprimanded according to his particular style of discipline; it was what men did. He wasn't abusing me when he hit me, he was merely 'keeping me in line'.

Wayne's violence had reached new levels. Simultaneously, the person I once was had disappeared to such an extent that I felt more like an extension of Wayne, there solely to ease his pain. And so, whatever he did to me, although on a deep level I knew was destroying me, seemed to be an acceptable response to my inability to make him happy.

Wednesday 12th January

Wayne didn't offer any apology for yesterday # and I didn't talk to him unless I had to. He was back to normal, everything was unchanged. He acted as if nothing had happened # and so I had to suppress my feelings as well or risk a repeat of yesterday if I said anything 'wrong'. My face was bruised and I couldn't turn my neck as it seemed to have seized up which made work hell.

Saturday 19th February

(Transcribed exactly as it was written without cleaning it up by adding punctuation as I wanted to try to convey the horrible reality of such abusive episodes.)

Horrible day, (an understatement, the following incident marked a new level of violence that resulted in my developing consistently high blood pressure and massively painful headaches) *I tried to avoid Wayne as he was in a bad mood, picky, then at lunchtime he didn't eat the meal I cooked him. He yelled at me and said I was lazy and his mother did more than me (he meant that she, not I, cooked meals he liked). I said: 'I'll never live up to her, she's perfect in your eyes and you should have married her.' He got up without saying a word to me just ran at me dragged me into the lounge room and pushed me to the ground so roughly I got a carpet burn on the elbow* (that burn was so deep it remained for months after the event). *The kids saw it all and panicked and I yelled at him for upsetting them. He ran into the bedroom and got the gun* (a 22-calibre rifle) *I was running to the front door saw he had the gun so I dropped to the floor in the family room crouching on my knees and covering my head with my hands and he said he was going to shoot me then and there. I said: 'Please don't do this in front of the kids,' and I begged him not to do it but if he was going to, to do it outside where the kids didn't have to see it. I believed he was going to shoot me and I was resigned to being killed. I was terrified yet a part of me just wanted to get it over with. I partly didn't care anymore because I really thought it was the end, he seemed to be so certain that he wanted me dead and that this was the best way to do it. He held the gun to my right temple for a while then kicked me and said: 'You're not worth a bullet.' I burst into tears then and went into the bedroom and he followed me still holding the gun so I went to leave and he slammed the door and wouldn't let me out, he punched me and kept pushing me with his chest on mine and sneering at me repeating everything I said in a sneering voice so I cried again and couldn't stop crying and told him to leave me alone. The girls were outside screaming for me over and over but they didn't open the door because he yelled at them 'not to open it or they'd get it'. After a little while they were quiet and they went into Charmaine's room. I didn't talk to him for the rest of the day and didn't tell anyone else what had happened* (who was there to tell?). *We went to work as usual as if this was an occurrence that didn't warrant any consequences. It's worse for the kids they will grow up mentally ill from this.*

Sunday 20th February

Wayne fought with me again before we went to work then as we were leaving the house he said: 'I shouldn't have punched you yesterday.' It seemed as if the gun violence had been wiped from his mind, dangerous to mention it again because even he must have realised the gravity of what he'd done and so it was easier to pretend the worst that had happened was his punching me. He said: 'I'll get on my hands and knees and grovel for you to stay. I love you more than anything, so stay.' After yesterday and knowing just how far he could go when he was angry, I was prepared to do anything to maintain the status quo. I was traumatised and couldn't think properly and the kids were worth anything rather than lose them if I left. Wayne would take them off me if I went away or else he'd shoot me. Wayne looked after the kids after work as I was so sick I had to sleep. Then I had the worst ever sinus attack when I woke up and my head pounded from unbearable pressure all night. (I didn't understand at the time that this was symptomatic of the trauma I had gone through, now I see the connection between the incident and my response to it.) *I slept on the lounge because I couldn't stop sneezing then I slept with Louise for comfort. My head ached all night and I woke up about ten times throughout the night.*

Soon after Wayne's holding a gun to my head incident I developed a pattern of experiencing migraines every two months, the severity of these resulting in me requiring hospitalisation and being attached to a drip for the headaches to abate. Coinciding with these migraines was hypertension, of which I still take medication to reduce the high blood pressure. On two occasions, after the gun episode, I collapsed in Wayne's parents' house prior to a work shift, with blood pressure so high the attending doctor initially thought that I was suffering from mini-strokes. I believe that the above health issues were in direct response to the trauma ensuing from the terror the gun at my head provoked in me.

As I write this entry for the book I am sickened by the fact that I stayed and STILL tried to right the wrongs of this relationship. How could I have possibly thought that Wayne could change after what he had done? By remaining I know he and I caused trauma for our children.

Monday 11th April

Nothing has changed, Wayne still moody and arguing. My head is still aching even when I got home tonight. Wayne and I argued then I cried so he got disgusted and went to bed because I couldn't stop crying and he yelled out: 'Shut up or I'll drive you through the wall.' I slept in Louise's bed and she slept on the bunk bed in Charmaine's room.

Tuesday 12th April

Argued all day. Louise and I went back to bed after Wayne took Charmaine down to the school bus and we didn't wake until 10.30am and my head ached all day again. I don't know if it's concussion (Wayne punched me in the head on Sunday) or stress. Wayne said he couldn't understand why I cry for what seems like nothing.

Saturday 7th May

Louise grabbed the scissors off the table during an argument with Charmaine and stabbed her in the chest just above the heart; the tip went through her clothes onto her skin but no bleeding luckily. It made me sick. Louise is often a violent child with Charmaine, but the scissors? This was the worst. It was so close to being serious. Wayne wasn't concerned and we had sex tonight as usual.

Friday 24th June

We went to St Peter's at 8.30am with Toby to clean windows during the school holidays and I was really sick and weak but that didn't stop Wayne getting his 'gutful' at Toby's after work. I lay outside in the Ute crying until he came back out. I suppose the infinitesimal spark of humanity left in him made him only stay for half an hour, then he sat up with Pam (we stayed at his parents the night) both of them talking loudly for another hour until 12.30am. Charmaine had thrown up in bed so she and Louise (the three of us were sharing the one bed) pushed over on to my side and pushed me out altogether so I slept on the floor all night hating everything in my life.

Monday 15th August

Wayne and Pam think I'm going through 'change of life' because I am so sick from headaches and depressed and 'moody' so they want me to see Dr Gladstone and have a hormone count done!

Thursday 18th August

Still have a migraine. Got Charmaine ready for school and walked her to the bus stop then came home and threw up breakfast. The pills Dr Gladstone gave me for headaches made me ill. Lay in bed all day again then got ready to go to town for the night run and I started vomiting non-stop. Still vomiting in town so Dr Gladstone came to Wayne's parents and took my blood pressure which was through the roof and he seemed to think I was exhibiting signs of stroke, poor eye focusing, etc., and he felt the swollen neck glands from the virus I've had for three weeks. I was in a mess. He drove me to Casualty while Wayne grudgingly went to work and I lay there for three hours while they gave me an EEG and a needle for nausea. I was put in East Wing Ward 22 and I stayed for two days for observation because it was thought that I might have had a mini stroke.

I was told while there that I had Carpel Tunnel Syndrome (a form of repetitive strain injury stemming from doing the same tasks over and over) in both hands, so much for being 'lazy at work'.

Saturday 20th August

I was allowed to leave hospital after breakfast and Wayne picked me up. He couldn't care less about my blood pressure being really high and my temperature also high, just said I could go to work today with him because he was 'buggered' and needed my help. So, I worked five and a half hours straight in one shift then went back for the night work after a coffee break.

Friday 26th August

Went to Dr Gladstone for testing on my thyroid gland and everything is fine and I am not going through menopause and he was annoyed that Wayne and Pam had even considered that my depression had anything to do with menopause. He said: 'What will they want next? Some test to see whether you're mentally unstable?'

Friday 2nd September

Charmaine begged to stay home from school yet again saying she was too sick. She is faking sickness a lot to stay at home (unlike myself, she really was pretending because as soon as she remained at home for the day she'd become energetic and ravenously hungry) and really unstable, crying all the time and yelling abuse at me constantly. When I told Wayne I was worried, he brushed it off and so did Pam who, when I appealed to her, trying to make sense of Charmaine's behaviour, put it down to my bad parenting skills.

Both Charmaine and Louise were exhibiting behaviours that I know now were symptomatic of the constant abuse their father perpetrated against me, their mother. Despite knowing about the girls' negative behaviours, the Family Court later said that Wayne had not directly abused them and although they'd witnessed him abusing me that did not indicate abusive parenting on his part. His actions would not have unduly hurt them provided they themselves weren't hit, the court maintained. It seemed that emotional abuse was not a factor in the children's behaviour. As long as he wasn't beating them and was limiting his violence toward me, he was in the eyes of the law an exemplary parent.

Sunday 4th September

After work Wayne said we'd stop off at a mate's place for a beer. I said I didn't want to with the kids, he screamed that I was a 'ball and chain' and he was 'master of the house' and we did what he said. # In the car on the way home I said that I was sick of the fighting and I wanted to leave and he said that I wasn't going anywhere. I said: 'You'd rather keep me here a prisoner knowing how I feel,' and he went off his brain and slapped me twice on the leg. (He often said that he couldn't control himself hitting me because of something I'd done to him, yet he didn't do it in front of others and made sure he didn't hit me in the face or on the body where it would show, and if seen by our bosses, might mean loss of contracts.) *Then he pulled my hair hard so my neck hurt and threw me out of the car halfway home. I walked back towards town not knowing what else to do and the poor kids were screaming as the car took off. I yelled out: 'Look after my kids, don't you hurt them.' After five minutes, he came back and pulled me into the car and kept yelling at me the rest of the way home and into the night until I felt that my head would explode.*

Tuesday 6th September

Wayne told me that ever since I'd said I was staying for the kids it had been eating away at him, that his mother had said the same thing to his father, and now I had said it and he kept thinking that I didn't care about him. Like a fool, I felt guilty and thought maybe that explained why he was so angry with me all the time lately and I apologised for making him feel bad.

Friday 9th September

My apology hasn't made any difference to him fighting with me. He picked on me again today and I cried, like I have every day this week.

Saturday 10th September

Wayne said he became confused and depressed when we fought and even though he wanted to make up to me he wouldn't because I'd think he was predictable and might take advantage of his weakness!

Deborah Thomson

Thursday 6th October

Wayne and I hardly talk to each other and I am so sick of it. No wonder I can't talk to anyone else. I'm out of practice after years of having no one to talk to and Wayne paying no attention to anything I say. # I feel worthless.

Tuesday 11th October

When I got back from taking Charmaine to the bus, Wayne said Nick (a friend of his) rang to say he was coming out tomorrow and that he was staying the week. I was upset because his friends could stay for a week without any problem; yet, my family were kicked out after three days at the house (they were 'bludgers' as far as Wayne was concerned) so Wayne kicked me hard in the foot to stop me talking and said I was a ball and chain. I was so sick of the same old cycle of fighting that I cried and said: 'I hate getting up every day to this. I've lost the will to live.' He said: 'So leave, but if you take the kids you'll get a bullet.' He would too because he doesn't care whether I want to stay married or not, it's all about what I can do for him, what he gets from me. The way he acts around Nick, I wouldn't be surprised if Wayne has gay tendencies and he's conflicted about his sexuality. His obsessive, possessive love for his mother can't be helping his mental state either.

Thursday 1st November

Wayne argued again with me this morning saying that I didn't do enough, he has to do everything, clean the house, look after the kids, and run the business ... I don't even give him enough sex! If the last were true it wouldn't be a wonder, his idea of foreplay being: 'Brace yourself Debbie.' I got a call from the school saying

Charmaine had to be picked up straight away because she had conjunctivitis and pupils with that condition weren't allowed at school. Wayne yelled at me as we were getting in the car to go to town for not telling the secretary off when she implied that I knew of this rule but had sent Charmaine to school anyway and it rapidly developed into screaming. I yelled at him to stop screaming at me over nothing and he pushed me so hard my head banged into the passenger window then he scratched my face so I turned around and went onto the front verandah to get away from him. He came after me screaming and it felt so like that time with the gun that I threw myself on the ground cowering. He picked me up and pretended (he later said) to throw me over the fence in a spear tackle head first, saying: 'I'm going to smash your head into the ground, you fucking bitch,' only I didn't think he was 'pretending' and grabbed the fence (it was wire) to stop myself going over it and cut my hands. He threw me over his shoulder and into the car instead of the fence and screamed at me all the way to town. Later a red weal came out on my face, my head ached from the impact with the window and I had a graze and bruises on my back. When we got to town Wayne talked and laughed with his family as if nothing had happened. I couldn't act like he did so just sat in the kitchen silent and twice Pam said to Wayne: 'What's wrong with her?' She completely ignored me as if it wasn't worth her asking if I was okay. Despite her rudeness to me Wayne thinks she's 'got all the class' and I was 'dragged up' by my parents.

The bottom line is 'I'll get a bullet' if I leave because I'm 'not ruining all the things' he's 'built up out on the farm'. When we got home tonight Wayne went to bed and I watched some television for a change, trying to digest another day of abuse.

Deborah Thomson

Wednesday 16th November

I slept in until 8am and Wayne whined about that. He was angry at me for talking to him about what happened yesterday. 'I forget immediately about fights,' he said, 'so you just have to go and remind me. No wonder I get mad at you, you nagger.' #

Sunday 20th November

Wayne yelled at the kids for making a noise when they were playing, so I said something to him, and it turned into a screaming match that went on all evening. He smashed another hole in one of the bedroom cupboards then at 2.30am he got up and turned the radio on so the music was really loud. He woke me so he could yell at me because he 'felt like it'. He said that he couldn't do anything he wanted anymore and asked me to leave because he didn't want me here anymore. Then, he said: 'Go to your drunken father and hippy mother.' He wouldn't stop yelling nor turn the music down so the kids were scared and crying and we all stayed up until 3.45am.

1995

Monday 23rd January

Took both the girls shopping and as usual it was stressful, they were so loud and fought the whole time. When we got back to Pam's, the kids could sense the tension in her home and, like they always do when around her, they went crazy and ran around the house yelling. As well, Wayne makes me feel physically sick in the stomach most of the time so no wonder I'm on edge, he just turns on me without warning and snarls at the smallest thing. # I did what he wanted tonight and had sex. #

Thursday 26th January

Pam has been away for two days. She got back tonight and rang us after work 'to see how my girls and my hard-working son are'. I didn't miss her aggression or depression, even Wayne was less stressed in her absence. However, as soon as he spoke to her on the phone he became agitated. He fought with me for the rest of the evening and we had to go to bed early. I had to wake him up at 11pm as he'd told me to do and masturbate him.

Saturday 11th February

We haven't fought this week but his animosity is just below the surface I can sense it.

Saturday 18th February

Good day at home no fighting.

Nothing more was written in this entry on that day because there was nothing to record unless of a violent nature; daily life consisted purely of abuse at home or work in town with the occasional free time to read if I wasn't expected that is, to sit with Wayne while he drank and continually spoke at me so that I wouldn't miss hearing his pearls of wisdom (a version of the world as he saw it and how hard done by he was in life).

Monday 6th March

Wayne is happily spending $1800 out of the house loan money to buy his old motor bike back but argued with me when I said I needed to start regularly taking blood pressure medicine for my hypertension. He said the tablets were not important, that he didn't believe I had high blood pressure and that doctors were always rorting people out of their money.

Wayne often taunted me about my health condition with comments such as: 'You don't have high blood pressure, the doctor's just saying that you're really sick so he can push drugs,' or 'You're a hypochondriac making out you're sick to get out of work.' Despite indisputable evidence to the contrary, he insisted that I was either pretending or forcing myself to have headaches and hypertension. As if the short hours off work when ill made up for the pain and distress I went through. As well as the pain, I had to deal with the extreme loneliness and vulnerability I felt whenever I was sick and virtually left to rot in a bedroom either at home or at Wayne's parents, without support or regular medication.

Thursday 9th March

Pam is fond of ordering everyone around especially me. She barks orders at me. I try to stay away from her and Wayne at the moment. I'm upset with everything and agitated and crying at the slightest thing. The kids wanting to play with me is the only time that I feel like I'm worth something to anyone.

Saturday 22nd April

Not much of a birthday, this day is never different to other days except Wayne looked after the kids while I slept in until 8am and they all said Happy Birthday, but no cake or being waited on or presents from them, except a bottle of Bourbon from Wayne after work, most of which he drank immediately after we got home. Luckily Mum and Grandma rang and said presents were on the way. They'd found time to send me something even after Mum had cracked two ribs and bruised her kidney from falling out of the bath and Grandma had had to look after her. Here, all I get is a bottle of Wayne's favourite alcohol.

Monday 8th May

Really depressed and frustrated, Wayne told me I can never take the kids up to visit my relatives without him and he never wants to leave town so I'll never be able to take the kids anywhere by myself. I'll never get out of this rut. I cried myself to sleep tonight.

Wednesday 31st May

Nothing changes, we get up early, go to work all day, get home late or on days off we stay home and Wayne gets drunk. We are in a well-heeled prison with no escape until death.

Thursday 3rd August

Wayne has been thinking of cutting back on work but Pam was on his back to keep existing contracts as soon as he told her this. She only worries that she'd lose the babysitting money we give her for the kids if we cut back. If we don't change the work routine and slow down the mad pace I'll have to do something because I can't handle this disgusting monotony, or his vicious mother controlling every decision we try to make because she thinks we are indebted to her for the babysitting.

Friday 4th August

Got dressed up and wore high heels and Wayne actually kissed me on the lips for almost as long as that filthy kiss he gave his mother on the lips to stop her yelling at him. A few weeks ago, Pam had been verbally abusing Wayne, calling him lazy for wanting to give up some work so he'd kissed her on the mouth, for minutes it seemed, so that she would stop talking. The kiss had looked obscene and very inappropriate but apart from me, no one else in the room thought it untoward. His and her obsession with each other goes unnoticed and unremarked in this family. I worry about Wayne being alone with her when he goes to town; she feeds him so much negativity and gloom and puts him down. He takes it out on me when he gets home because he's so wrapped in her and can't face her being wrong, so the blame for her actions falls on me.

Saturday 19th August

Usual stressed day at home. Wayne yelled at the poor kids the entire day because they were sick with the flu and wouldn't settle.

Sunday 27th August

We had a huge fight over Pam and the influence she has over Wayne. He is on her wavelength and sees my criticism of her, no matter how slight as devastating so he reacts badly to what I say about her. Had to masturbate him tonight and his penis is black with bruises from last night's masturbating. That's what happens when it's all we do just about every night.

Monday 28th August

Wayne went to work early and got back at 10.30am. He said he was selling the Jackaroo and buying his father's Valiant (an ugly petrol-eating car, so ugly that once we'd bought it, the kids would make us drop them around the corner from their school rather than be seen alighting from it). As soon as I voiced doubts about his wisdom in buying that car he got this 'spoilt brat' tone, the one he'd used all his life so that his mother would give him anything he'd wanted. She has a lot to answer for, the way she brought him up and now she's doing the same damage to my kids. He screamed at me, grabbed me by the scruff of the neck and shook me then dropped me to the floor. He was furious and left the house then came back and we made up. Thank God, no more fighting.

Wayne had a massive sense of entitlement fuelled by his upbringing, with Pam satisfying his every whim. He'd also often witnessed his father verbally and physically abusing his mother; his father had been raised to resolve disputes with his fists so it was normal for him to bring such strategies into his own marriage. His parents' behaviours may have had a strong influence on the man he became and helped to explain his abusive behaviours; however, it didn't excuse his abuse.

Tuesday 29th August

It's so good to stay at home for a change. Am coming out of that bad mood where I'm scared all of the time with everything getting on my nerves. I am by myself right now without Wayne talking constantly in my ear like he often does when he's home. I've never met anyone who can talk as much as he can, especially about himself.

When he wasn't manic and talking at me constantly, he'd avoid speaking to me and sit in a brooding silence for days at a time, only yelling or screaming when the mood took him.

Saturday 2nd September

Good day, hardly any yelling from Wayne and the kids acted better for that.

As discussed earlier in the book, Wayne's good behaviour was a classic symptom of the *cycle of violence* which looks like this: explosion-remorse phase, honeymoon phase, build-up phase, stand-up phase, explosion and the cycle is complete **(www.communities.qld.gov.au, 2014)**. Every time Wayne was in the pursuit and honeymoon phases (he skipped remorse), I was so naïve, gullible and tending to see good in everyone that I would justify his explosions and think that this time he was going to stop the abuse. I accepted his negative behaviours and became incredibly adept at explaining them away or excusing them. I continually analysed his abuse in terms of how I could fix it, not how he could.

Thursday 7th September

Cleaned the art museum then rushed the shopping so Wayne wouldn't get uptight about lunch being late. I never have time to do anything else downtown: bar shopping for food, because I have to hurry back to him.

He later told me that he'd arranged with Nick (his best friend who idolised Wayne) to follow me every time I was downtown on my regular Thursday shopping trips and report back to Wayne, everywhere I went and everyone I spoke to. This revelation came as a shock to me and it started me wondering just what other underhanded thing Wayne might have done during our marriage. Wayne's spying also incensed me greatly because, unlike him having occasionally stayed in town overnight then taunting me about women he'd met and hinting that he'd slept with, I had never done anything to cause him to doubt my fidelity and loyalty to him.

Friday 15th September

Wayne fought all morning with me, picking and being sarcastic when he wasn't raising his voice to me. I can't talk to him at all unless I'm talking about things he wants to talk about. Pam is threatening to move out and quit working for us AGAIN and Wayne took it out on me after he became stressed talking to his mother.

Sunday 17th September

Wayne is cold one day, then, once in a blue moon, he'll say that what we've got is precious, that we can't lose it. When he says that, I always think that he's changed. # Every time I fall for his good moods, after the bad moods. I begin to hope that things will improve when he says that I'm perfect and the best wife a man could want.

I realised while writing this book that he never said *he'd improve*. It was always things like: 'We have a special relationship', 'We have too much to lose to break up,' 'You are the most important thing to me'—words that did not assign responsibility for his abuse or tell me he was going to change for the better or even that he felt any remorse for the dreadful violence he'd perpetrated against me.

Friday 8th December

Wayne was really snapping at me tonight so I assumed he didn't want sex. He always snaps at me first then says the fight is my fault because he takes offence at something I've said, when all I am doing is defending myself in response to his abuse!

As well as dealing with Wayne, his mother featured as a major player in our lives and the co-dependent relationship between son and mother coloured mine and Wayne's relationship. The more she insinuated herself into our marriage the greater was Wayne's level of abuse towards me. It felt more like a ménage à trois, with the three of us having to wend our way through a minefield of dysfunctional personalities. Unfortunately, our children were part of the dysfunction, as children always are in such situations, this dysfunction often resulting in generational abuse that has the potential to ruin countless lives.

1996

Friday 5th January

Went to hospital for the clinic appointment at 12.15pm. Charmaine was with me for the ultrasound on the baby. (I was pregnant again and this was the five-monthly check-up.) Looking at the screen, I asked where the heartbeat was. Dr Wilco said nothing, he looked for ten minutes then asked me if I'd been nauseous, had a high temperature or respiratory problems (I had caught the flu from Pam a while ago and had had those symptoms) then he said, in front of poor Charmaine: 'I am sorry to have to tell you this but your baby has died, there's no heartbeat, the head is the size of a twelve-week baby and the head structure is wrong.' Wayne didn't say anything when I told him. We went to work, did the art museum then stayed in town at his father's (Pam had moved out into a unit of her own) *because I was too upset to go home.*

Saturday 6th January

I was put on a drip to induce labour then had a curette after the baby was born to remove all remaining traces of the little girl. I called her Samantha, she was perfectly formed but had no brain due to anencephaly I was told, and this is what had caused her to die. I had been carrying her in that state for weeks. I have to stay in hospital overnight.

I speak matter-of-factly in this entry but the devastation I felt after yet another miscarriage was so deep I could neither voice it, nor write it down. I could only repress my despair as I had done many times previously whenever something traumatic occurred.

Monday 8th January

Went to work in town at a quarter to four in the morning whether I was up to it or not. Wayne let me have the rest of the day off after the morning shift.

Monday 15th January

Wayne is angry because we can't have sex. We did St Peter's Year 7 block windows, which took three hours, while Pam babysat the kids and filled them with soft drink. I was really depressed today and started bleeding heavily again after I'd completely stopped yesterday. I masturbated Wayne tonight.

Friday 26th January

Wayne went on all day about buying a Harley motor bike after seeing one in Tamblyn, he wants to spend $19,000, all our savings, even woke me up in the middle of last night to talk about the bike. We argued most of the day and he said I was 'so selfish', as if I was spending the money on myself when all I want to do is pay off the loan on the house, God forbid! While we were cleaning Vinnies (we'd recently gained a contract to clean St Vincent De Pauls) *he threw all the cleaning gear in the gutter outside the shop then screamed like an imbecile at nothing in particular. When* *we got into the car he screamed at me and said that if he wanted a fucking bike then he was getting a fucking bike and no one was stopping him.*

Wednesday 7th February

Wayne went out last night and said he'd run into an old girlfriend and today he's got what looks like a love bite on his arm. He says it's a bruise but it's in the shape of a mouth and has bite marks around it.

Wayne constantly accused me of having affairs with his friends, even saying that our girls had different fathers, yet during our entire relationship I remained loyal. I had strong reason to believe that he did not pay me the same compliment.

Thursday 8th February

Wayne had the worst screaming fit in my presence mostly to do with my reluctance to spend our savings on such a superfluous item as a motorbike. During this outburst, he called me a fucking halfwit.

Wednesday 14th February

The kids are still getting on Wayne's nerves because they wouldn't be quiet, even after he'd screamed at them yesterday to quieten them down. He sits in the kitchen every night away from us and says he'd be at the 'pub' if we lived in town, as if he's got the right to forget about us and go out to get away, when he holds us prisoners here. We are literally held captive, he holds the car keys and the front gate is locked so I couldn't take the kids anywhere without him.

Deborah Thomson

Saturday 24th February

Wayne screamed at me yesterday then wonders why I'm cool towards him. Anyway, I look so ugly I can't bring myself to be the femme fatale Wayne expects me to be, so I come across as hard. Not so hard, however, that I didn't have to masturbate him tonight.

Tuesday 27th February

We had another loud night at home with Wayne yelling and the kids yelling at each other. I am feeling really down lately, almost blacking out with depression.

I was fractured, with no idea who I was or what I represented, the result of having had to deal with Wayne's moods for so long. I did not know how to be introspective, nor did I have the time. Most of my time was taken up with watching Wayne, trying to figure out his next move, to the extent that I disappeared as a person in my own right. I now know that sacrificing myself was debilitating for my psyche, and to have allowed another person such control over everything I said, did and felt, was soul-destroying.

Tuesday 26th March

Wayne said that work was good for the soul; however, his idea of work is based on his mother's opinion that anyone who doesn't work all day every day is not contributing to a marriage. They both think that you're only worthy if you do hard physical labour every day. How do I fit into this ridiculous notion of someone's worth? Wayne and I had a huge shouting fight over this and didn't talk all night.

Thursday 28th March

Had a huge argument tonight, one of the worst we've had in months. I told Wayne he was a hick so he grabbed my arm and twisted it to the point where I thought it would break but it just bruised all over. I screamed at him to get lost for hurting me like that. My screaming angered him so much he drove the car down the paddock as fast as he could with it fish tailing, then came back and went to bed slamming the door. I sat in the lounge room shaking and was still awake at 11pm. For once Wayne didn't scream at me to come to bed.

After years of bearing the brunt of his abuse, I had reached the point of no return, occasionally reacting to his violence in ways that often incited him to further violence. But by now I was beyond caring, so depressed and desperate that it appeared the only option left to me was to respond to his screaming in kind, in the hope that my resistance would cause him to desist from abusing me. Of course, my responses were limited to the verbal, not the physical. I was still frightened of his physical strength. I did not use this form of resistance for much longer after the above incident as arguing with him did not make any difference to the frequency of his abusive behaviour. So, yet another strategy that I'd hoped would end his abuse: others being: appealing to his better nature, the silent treatment, leaving the room he was in, and now yelling back at him during arguments, proved to be as ineffectual.

Friday 29th March

Argued again all morning until we went to Charmaine's Easter parade where he said he loved me. We had sex tonight so that we could, as Wayne put it, 'make up properly'.

Thursday 18th April

Wayne screamed at the kids tonight for nothing at all so I took them to bed at 6.30pm.

Saturday 20th April

Wayne was really drunk. I told him off for screaming at the kids at bath time for wanting to have the heater on. While I was getting dinner, I told him off again for being a maniac, screaming at the kids for nothing and frightening them. As I was carrying two plates of eggs on toast to the table he tipped them up and they landed all over my front. I dropped the plates in surprise and they smashed, food everywhere so I took the kids into Louise's bedroom, away from him, then cleaned the mess up. He went to bed then threw up all over the floor in the toilet and couldn't move from the floor where he was lying, so I had to clean that up as well.

Saturday 25th May

I was sick from a headache all day and had diarrhoea and stomach cramps so when Wayne dragged me to him to start with some sex I told him that he was only interested in the bottom half of me and didn't care that I was sick. He got really cranky and threw me off him onto the floor.

Saturday 1st June

Charmaine had her friend Tiffany stay over and both woke Wayne up when they were debating about who got the top bunk in Charmaine's room, so he screamed at Charmaine to 'shut the fuck up' and scared Tiffany so much she never stayed again.

Sunday 9th June

Huge day of cleaning, windows at Kentish House (our contract) that went from 7am until noon then dropped in to Barry's to see the kids off to a party at Wayne's Aunty Denise's. We didn't go to it as we had to go back to work. Over to St Peter's to clean the Year 9 building then home at 5pm to take Charmaine to Pizza Hut (she'd won a voucher from school for reading) for a pizza and dessert. I stayed with her while Wayne went to Impies but we missed out on dessert because Wayne turned up much earlier than he said he would and didn't want to wait any longer. We were only there for 20 minutes!

Tuesday 16th July

Wayne was still as angry as he had been last night and went on about his porridge being cold. I said something he mustn't have liked and he said I was to blame for all the arguments, I was the cranky one, and he got up from the table swinging his fists at me and screaming. Charmaine was crying hysterically. When Louise and I walked her to the school bus we stayed down there for an hour hoping that Wayne would cool off. Instead he came looking for us and started screaming again.

Wednesday 17th July

I was arguing with Wayne this morning because he yelled at the kids for nothing and for snapping at me in a sarcastic voice all the time. I then figured I'd stay away from him to stop him arguing but he followed me around talking non-stop.

Keeping out of his way during and after arguments, was proving to be useless.

Sunday 28th July

Wayne is constantly yelling at the kids and me, he hasn't let up for days. It's so bad I'm in tears most of the time and a nervous wreck.

Thursday 1st August

I'm suffering from headaches most days. Pam said I brought it on myself by stressing so we ended up arguing. She complained to Wayne asking him to do something about my arguing with her and saying that he should be able to control his wife better than he did. The headache from this morning was still there later making me feel sick. It was hell working through it so I had to lie down at Pam's in between shifts and she complained to Wayne that I was lazy because I didn't help her cook dinner.

Saturday 3rd August

This headache won't go away, so bad I lay in bed all day and Wayne said I was a 'waste of space'.

Saturday 31st August

Terrible day, I spoke to Wayne about being too hard on the kids. He'd been screaming at them so much that I was scared he might lose control and hurt them. He argued then went to bed for the day. When he got up Louise was crying because of her chest infection so Wayne yelled again about the noise. When I said, I'd leave and take the kids so that he'd have peace and quiet he said: 'You can't leave, you have no idea what I feel about you, do you?'

Truer words were never said: I really had no idea what he felt.

Friday 4th October

I woke at 4am heart pounding and scared from screaming because of a nightmare, during which I'd told Wayne to get lost. The noise woke him and he screamed at me for waking him so I slept out on the lounge for the rest of the night.

Even today I still have nightmares where I wake up yelling in fear from being attacked by Wayne in my dreams. The difference between having nightmares then and nightmares now, is that I awake frightened and am comforted, not as in the past, half-strangled in anger by Wayne for waking him.

Friday 18th October

Wayne and Pam got together to discuss when I should go off work (I was six months into another pregnancy), and they decided for me that I should finish in three weeks and she'd take over my work. I worry that their working together will mean that they spend more time with each other. Whenever this has happened in the past, she's taken over his life and Wayne becomes even more horrible to me.

Saturday 19th October

Had to have sex with Wayne to stop him yelling at me. Sometimes I hate him so much for being sarcastic and arrogant, just like Pam is to me. I can't escape his sarcasm and arrogance at home and have to live with the same from his mother while we are in town.

Deborah Thomson

Monday 21st October

Saw the doctor at 11.30 for the fortnightly pregnancy check-up and my blood pressure is high so I will probably be induced two weeks earlier than the due date, as was the case with my other pregnancies. Pam is her usual domineering self and Wayne talks to me in exactly the same way she does to me, yet he won't talk to her like that. We went to St Peters after lunch to do the afternoon work.

Tuesday 22nd October

Rotten day with Charmaine (now seven years of age) abusing me like her father does, yelling and talking rudely to me like I'm a dog. I'm sick of her fighting with me. I now have the two of them to deal with at home. Louise is the only one who, like me, doesn't want to make waves.

Wednesday 30th October

Wayne has been fighting with me every day this week and the only break I get from it is when he goes to town without me. Then I get threatening behaviour from Charmaine when she gets home from school so I'm going crazy with depression. Having absolutely no one to talk to about how I feel is how I imagine it'd be, stuck in solitary confinement.

Thursday 7th November

Deidre (my sister-in-law) dropped photos of the girls into her mother's home for me to collect. Pam happened to be at Bet's (Deidre's mother) at the time so took them without asking if I minded and kept them, even though they were intended for me.

Wayne couldn't see that she'd done anything wrong and told me off for being selfish for wanting the photos. His mother can do no wrong in his opinion and I feel like I am constantly hitting my head against a wall when I try to get some respect from them and they either act like I don't exist or put me down. When it's in front of the kids, Charmaine copies Wayne and Pam. I have no one to turn to and it's getting me down, to the point where I wish for death.

Saturday 16th November

We'd gone to a 21st tonight and Wayne got so drunk he urinated in the cupboard in his parent's spare room then threw up for an hour and kept falling over on his way to the toilet. He screamed abuse at me when I told him about the cupboard and called me a fucking liar.

Friday 29th November

Booked a place in the maternity ward for the day I'd be induced then dropped in to Wayne's parents (Pam had returned to Barry) while Wayne and Pam went to work. Pam came back at 4.30pm. She'd left Wayne at work because he was 'such a pig to work with' and she said that she would no longer work for us. She can't cope with the same work that I had to when seven months pregnant! I think she is angling to babysit fulltime for us but there is absolutely no chance I'll let that happen. (As if I have any say.)

It was a year of poor health for the kids with frequent chest/ear infections and vomiting. I was experiencing migraines, skin rashes, high blood pressure, sleep deprivation and recurring nightmares that left me shaking uncontrollably;

symptomatic, I now understand, of the constant tension from living in a highly stressful environment where nothing made sense. The rules of polite society were non-existent and love for family was expressed through violence. I often felt as though I alone knew what altruistic love was, everyone else around me expressed 'love' according to self-gain. This confused and upset me. Feeling as I did greatly alienated me from my husband, his family and the children. Naturally, given my thinking at that time, I laid the fault upon myself for the alienation. I blamed myself for not conforming to their values, for not being more like them.

1997

Wednesday 1st January

I've been in hospital for a week. Wayne has hardly been to see me and when I rang him at home tonight he sounded really drunk. He had probably drunk everything he could find in the house judging by his voice.

Thursday 2nd January

I'm not due to be induced until the 18th but they want me to stay in hospital because my blood pressure keeps climbing and I am now on six tablets a day, the highest dose I'm allowed to have. Wayne brought the kids up before lunch and they were so loud fighting that he yelled at them and then took them home. The whole time he was here he kept saying he was lonely, couldn't handle work and having to drive back to the property at night, and for me to hurry up and have the baby as he couldn't cope. Wayne saw the doctor while he was visiting me and talked the hospital into letting me leave. They did, on the proviso that I stay in town and not in the bush where they couldn't keep an eye on me. Once I was out of the hospital Wayne disregarded their advice and took me back to the property.

Deborah Thomson

Saturday 18th January

I had contractions all last night but I'm only 3cm dilated this morning so they said they'd induce me and asked whether I'd like to be induced at 6am or 9am. I chose the latter hoping that the contractions would get stronger in the meantime so I could avoid being put on the drip for just one of my labours. Wayne arrived at 7am and yelled at me for not taking the drip at 6am as he didn't have time to wait around while I had the baby. Starting the labour earlier would have meant the baby would be born earlier and he could take off sooner, he argued. Kirra was born at 12.03pm, three weeks premature and only weighing 5lbs 8ozs. No sooner was she born, Wayne voiced his disappointment that he'd been given yet another girl.

Saturday 1st February

Mum and Grandma had come to stay for a few days to help me with Kirra. I was having problems with her not feeding, because she was so small, and was dead tired from trying to feed her on the hour every night since I'd brought her home. Still Wayne argued with me for not cooking lunch so I had to cook it. Then he got drunk and yelled at Grandma, Mum and I because he thought that Kirra felt too hot and that we should have done something about it seeing 'we were home all day doing fuck all'. Unfortunately, Grandma answered him saying that Kirra was cool enough, she'd been a nurse so knew something about babies and Wayne screamed at her saying that she knew nothing and to shut up. He told her that she shouldn't backchat him and that he 'could teach her a thing about manners' then called her an old lady who was out of touch. He screamed that she should keep her opinions regarding babies to herself because his mother knew more about raising children than she ever would. Grandma burst into tears and had to take a heart tablet because she was so upset by Wayne's screaming she felt as if she could have a heart attack. Wayne then turned on Mum saying it was disgusting that a fifty-year-old was being looked after by an eighty-year-old (in reality Mum had moved in with Grandma so she could care for her in her vulnerable state) and that she was heartless for taking advantage of Grandma. Wayne and I then fought in the laundry and outside the shed over the way he spoke to my family. He went up to the bedroom and cried, blaming his outburst on the recent death of his grandmother. (It was always something external that caused him to be abusive. He never took personal responsibility for his actions and only apologised for the hurt he inflicted on others when he thought he could benefit from any apology he made. He blamed everything and everyone, other than himself, for his anger. He was never remorseful for the destruction he caused either.) *There was no excuse for him upsetting my grandmother to the point where she'd almost had a heart attack and when Mum said that they were never coming back here again I knew that they meant it. They had every reason not to return.*

Friday 28th March

Wayne and I had a bad fight this morning and he told me to get out. When I said, I wouldn't leave without the kids he said: 'Right that's it, you're getting a bullet,' and he went up to the bedroom where he kept the gun. I could hear him going into the roof space where he kept the guns so I ran outside and hid in the top paddock where I could watch the house. He came outside looking for me with the rifle in his hand so I stayed hidden until I saw him drive off to town. I was outside for an hour and worried about Kirra inside but she was asleep when I went back in.

The occurrence of incidents such as the one above reinforced the isolation I experienced living so far from town and neighbours. This isolation allowed Wayne the opportunity to scream, fire a rifle if he'd wanted or rampage as loudly as he felt the need to without fear of being heard or of anyone outside the home intervening. He had complete control and I was powerless while I chose to remain with him.

Tuesday 22nd April

Some birthday ... no one remembered it to begin with and even when Charmaine saw the date and realised what day it was, she only said: 'It's your birthday today, huh.' Wayne didn't remember until Grandma rang to wish me happy birthday and when I told her that no one here cared she said that was awful and Mum cried on the phone for me. I bogged the car picking the girls up from the school bus and when Wayne found out after he came home he screamed at me for being 'a useless cunt'. He threw the can of Jim Beam and Cola he'd bought me for forgetting my birthday at my face and I cried for the fifth time that day. He took the tractor down to pull the car out of the hole it was in and bogged the tractor before he managed to get the car out.

Sunday 4th May

Wayne got drunk and carried on about how much I meant to him then during a discussion at dinner about my driving skills he said:

'Put the car in neutral before you start it,' in such a patronizing tone that I said: 'Don't worry, I'm not an idiot, you don't have to tell me.' He exploded because I apparently dared not to listen to the great man's advice, screaming that I needed all the advice I could get I was so fucking stupid. He ran at me then, punching his fist into the palm of his other hand and screaming: 'Stop me hitting you, go on.' I yelled in fear which seemed to anger him more so he grabbed my arm and yanked it behind my back until it felt like it was going to break. Then he dragged me into the lounge room and threw me on the floor. The kids were screaming during all of this so I stayed on the floor until he went to bed, hoping that lying still and quiet would defuse the situation. I slept on the sofa with Kirra and cried during the night waking Wayne and he screamed at me to shut up. He told me that I had no right to cry because I had brought it on myself (meaning the fight).

Monday 5th May

Wayne continued arguing saying it was my fault that we fought # and I told him to stop drinking and going crazy.

Thursday 22nd May

Wayne yelled at me this morning and then said it was me who started the fights. # Then he carried on about how much he had to do for me, drive me around in town (all I do when downtown is shop for food and pay bills) clean the house and so on. I told him to stop talking and leave me alone so he became even angrier and tipped Louise's breakfast (I'd been preparing breakfast for everyone) all over the sink and the floor and screamed like a manic madman.

I only have to say one thing on the wrong day and he screams at me, ruining my life for days. He never says it's his fault, he always has a reason to get angry: I 'nag' him or I 'demand' too much and so on and so on. The kids are seeing terrible fights but I can't leave. I'm worried that he'll kill me or take the kids away so I just go along between the fights hoping that something will change. Had a rotten headache after the fighting but couldn't go to bed until all the jobs were done.

At the time, I also wrote: '*He is working too hard but he won't give any contracts away, maybe that makes him so irritable.*' Like Wayne, I too made excuses for his behaviour; justifying his actions, always thinking that it was something other than himself that caused his anger. So often I would diminish his abusive behaviour, for example by saying he was irritable rather than the screaming lunatic he in reality was.

Monday 21st July

It was a good day until Wayne came home. He was in a bad mood and would have taken it out on me no matter what. He said I didn't give him any support, then he pushed me around when I said that I didn't get any support from him especially when his mother abused me. (He always stuck up for her yet never did for me.) I said that she couldn't do any wrong in his eyes and it hurt that he never supported me when she argued with me. He stopped pushing me and I went up to the bedroom to pack and leave to stop the fighting, because Kirra was screaming. She was so scared of Wayne. He came after me and pushed me to the ground and I grazed my elbow on the wooden floor. I started crying and the kids were crying in the hallway. I went outside the house to give him a chance to calm down and I heard him coming out after me. I turned around and he had the axe in his hands and this horrible look on his face. I'd never seen his eyes so devoid of expression as they were just then. I collapsed on the ground and grabbed his legs and begged for my life. He stood over me for a few minutes saying in a really dead voice: 'Should I use this? Why not? There's no one here to see me do it,' then went back inside locking the front door so I couldn't come inside. I cried and knocked on the door to be let in because I didn't want him inside with the kids, but he kept telling me to shut up he wasn't going to let me in. I sat by the door for an hour and the kids let me inside after he'd gone to bed.

After I'd gotten over the terror of this incident I was so angry at Wayne for reducing me to a blubbering heap, begging for my life, that I wrote in my diary he was a 'fucking filthy pig'. It was the only recourse I had to punish him for what he'd done.

Once again, readers may wonder at my stupidity for staying after yet another horrible incident, but by now one violent abusive event was bleeding into the rest. The abuse was becoming more violent and frequent, to such an extent that *I began to feel grateful to Wayne for not killing me* during these fights. As long as I remained alive I thought I could handle whatever he did to me, until I could leave and take the girls with me.

Tuesday 22nd July

The kids were upset at school today. I tried to talk to Wayne about how sickening his behaviour is for them and his response was to threaten that he wouldn't come home tonight. (Electricity hadn't been connected to our new house. We had a generator and solar panels for power. If he didn't come home at night to turn the generator on we'd be in darkness.) *I know he will come home because he was acting like he'd forgotten about last night, until I mentioned it. I also knew he expected me to forget it as well because he said that what happened last night was nothing, I wasn't hurt. To him, threats of violence were not the same as actual violence, that if physical abuse didn't occur then it wasn't a problem and shouldn't be for me either. He said: 'I'm not a typical guy who beats up women. I lost my temper, that's all.' # I told him that I wouldn't stand for his behaviour but what's the use? I am standing for it by not leaving, however I can't disrupt the kids' lives yet.*

By this stage, when I threatened to leave I was willing to go without the girls and return for them with help from someone outside of the family. I hadn't formulated any sort of plan for leaving. However, I no longer wanted to keep our family intact. His violence was escalating: he hadn't killed me yet but I sensed that this was becoming a distinct possibility and I could finally see that the children's erratic behaviours stemmed from the constant turmoil in the house.

Wednesday 6th August

Wayne stayed home today. We aren't getting on at all; the kids are ruining his life, he said.

Following these words, I had written in my diary: *'What's really doing it is he works too hard.'* It seemed that neither of us understood the dynamics of domestic violence. We both blamed external factors for his violence. For me, it was incomprehensible that a human being could act the way Wayne did without having a very good reason outside of his psyche, to account for his behaviour. Neither of us realised that his abuse was the same as domestic violence. Even had we recognised this, Wayne still wouldn't have been prepared to examine the real reasons for his abuse.

Thursday 7th August

I hate cleaning in town and I hate the monotony of my life, it's so boringly mind-numbingly predictable. I never know when he's going to blow up and when he does I hate him for days, it's always the same.

Tuesday 12th August

It was a usual day at home. Wayne was fighting with me however we came to a truce later. What a merry-go-round it is, everything is rotten one day, worse the next.

Tuesday 19th August

Louise vomited after breakfast and kept vomiting, bringing up blood as well so we took her to town to the doctors. He said she was a very sick girl with one of her lungs fully clogged with mucus. He gave her strong drugs to stop the vomiting and ordered allergy tests.

It transpired, after extensive testing, that Louise was allergic to sugar and yeast. She had to cut out all foods with these ingredients for the short term. We were told that if she adhered to the diet for a few months, the number of chest infections she'd been experiencing would reduce dramatically. The diet lasted for three weeks until Pam who'd complained throughout of the cost of the diet while babysitting Louise, returned to giving her sugary junk food in large quantities. As she was still babysitting the girls every second day I could not control what food she gave them, no matter how I argued with her on this point. Louise continued to have chest infections and I, metaphorically speaking, continued to hit my head on that brick wall while ever I had no say over the raising of the children.

Friday 22nd August

Wayne is fighting with me AGAIN over Pam's parenting style with our children. We sorted it out (he yelled at me to 'shut the fuck up') and he told me that I had to ignore his moods: 'They mean shit all.'

Sunday 31st August

I was shocked to find out that Princess Diana was in a car accident and died from a massive lung haemorrhage today. Tonight, we all watched football and Wayne got drunk as usual. He thought that I was 'nagging' him about getting a bore put in for extra water so he stood up and screamed at me, then purposely knocked one of the cupboards in the lounge room over and Kirra cried in fear. Wayne then knocked the ironing board over (I'd been ironing while watching TV) nearly hitting Louise, then he told me to get fucked and stormed off to bed. I cried and cried and the girls were so good, they sat with me hugging me. It is so awful for them seeing this behaviour.

Saturday 1st November

The kids and I were going out for the first time in months so Wayne picked a huge fight with me. He does that whenever we go somewhere because he hates having to take us out and wants us to hate it too, making us as miserable as possible by arguing before we go. He called me a bitch and the kids cried but we went to Urindy anyway. (The day out entailed going to our block of land in town and watching Wayne mow it.) Wayne let me drive halfway home but criticised my driving the entire time. Charmaine said: 'You're a good driver Mummy.' She's been so understanding lately and makes me feel needed when Wayne makes me so sad.

Monday 3rd November

Wayne's still fighting with me badly, so much so tonight that I went out onto the verandah and cried for ages then I slept in the lounge room. The kids cried during his yelling so I said I'd leave if it would stop him fighting but I can't keep saying that without actually going, not that my threats make a difference. Wayne called me hysterical and a 'queero'. He has no understanding of suffering especially if it isn't physical.

Tuesday 4th November

Slept in the lounge room again tonight because Wayne is still fighting with me. I don't want to have anything to do with him. Luckily, he hasn't wanted sex the last few days. The kids have been uncontrollable because of the constant fighting they've witnessed.

Wednesday 5th November

Wayne made up as best he could only because he wanted sex, so we did it. He thought that by being nice to me it would be enough to elicit my good will towards him. He didn't notice my lack of interest during the act.

Friday 14th November

Kirra is having a week of developments, she learnt how to throw a ball to me, climbed the stairs to the pantry and hallway and she is now walking in the walker. Despite these milestones, Wayne was angry as usual and we had a huge fight this morning. He threw his jumper in my face then came up really close and screamed in my left ear so that it rang, then kicked the lounge and ripped the fabric. He went outside for a moment then came back in to talk to me as if nothing had happened. #

I had brought another child into this family without considering the repercussions. My motivation behind continuing to fall pregnant was to create something worthwhile and beautiful which I believed would, through my love, insulate us from Wayne's violence. I am so different now to the person I was then. I find it hard to describe my frame of mind during those years or the thoughts that led me to believe that any child born into that abusive environment would be insulated from Wayne's violence towards me. I thought that I could keep them from being hurt and that having children was part of the direction my life was heading then. I had sincerely believed that Wayne and I would remain together, when I fell pregnant each time. I did not envisage us separating until much later after the last child was born so, before my knowing that it was possible to leave, it seemed to me that children were a natural progression of our marriage and part of life's plan. However, loneliness played a part too. The idea that loneliness was a factor in my having children to this man is something that continues to cause me great distress. When I think of the hurt I had inflicted on the girls by bringing them into that environment, partly because of a hole in my life at the time, I feel sick to my core.

1998

Sunday 27th March

Wayne was rude to me at the art museum, saying I was ugly with teeth like a heroin addict (meaning that they were small he explained later) so I argued with him and cried in bed tonight. He was angry because I wouldn't sleep with him after he'd run me down all day. I slept in the lounge room to get some peace.

Monday 28th March

He continued fighting with me and denigrating my looks so I cried in the car on the way to Urindy. Wayne was still fighting with me when we got home tonight and he drank a lot of alcohol in a very short time. In the hallway, he kept screaming at me then he grabbed me and threw me around. I fell against the back door, the handle of which as it slammed open, left a hole in the hall wall. Wayne punched another hole in the wall beside it in fury then grabbed my shoulders and shook me. I kicked and scratched him to get him away from me, and he bled from a scratch on the bridge of his nose. (I'd accidentally scratched the scar he'd gotten on his nose from tackling me in the road, August 1986.) *I was terrified of him and kept scratching his face to defend myself from his violence. He threw me down on the wooden floor and dragged me by the hair along the hallway. I got a graze on my shoulder and bruises from being dragged and grazes on my elbows from being pushed hard into the back door. He pulled me up and yelled that he was going to throw me down the back stairs so I screamed in fright, then he really did throw me off the back verandah down five steps and I landed on my head. I had a bruised head and grazed forehead from that, my neck hurt and bruises came out on my shoulders where he'd grabbed me hard and I had a sore throat from being half choked before I was thrown off the verandah. I tried to come back inside and he kept stopping me with his fists up to fight me so I sat on the outside steps defeated. He went in and got a beer, brought it out and poured it over my head. I flipped and screamed like an animal, so loud that I was spitting and my voice was hoarse for two days after. My eyes were bulging, I'd lost control of my sanity and the years of pent up hurt and frustration came to a head. I could feel myself losing my grip on my mind and it frightened me. Wayne locked the back door so I couldn't come back inside but by then I was so sick from the fight I sat in the dark, numb from tiredness. The kids were screaming at Wayne to let me in and he screamed at them saying that he'd cut their hands off if any of them tried to unlock the door for me. Eventually he calmed down, Louise let me in and later Wayne wanted sex. I think the violence had turned him on. I refused because I was beyond caring* what he did to me (as I have said before, one of only a handful of refusals while we were together).

Sunday 24th May

Ever since that fight in March, we've had an uneasy truce where Wayne has only yelled at me, nothing physical; however,

Charmaine has become so abusive to me that I'm despairing that she'll ever love me like she does her father. Louise was so sick and headachy today that she didn't eat all day. Wayne said that he couldn't live without me, being alone 'would mean nothing'. He thinks that by saying this it makes up for his arguing and I'll be a better wife to him. Then he never helps me with Kirra's crying, instead he yells at me to go and sleep in Charmaine's room with Kirra so he won't be woken up by her crying and I wonder why I should try to be a better wife.

Wednesday 17th June

Still sick from a virus I caught while in Coonawarra (where I went with Charmaine who was competing in state orienteering) with diarrhoea and vomiting. Wayne screamed at Kirra so I took her into Charmaine's room where we stayed all morning, both of us crying.

Friday 19th June

I was so sick and not getting any sympathy from Wayne so I told him that I had nothing to live for. He got angry and said that he'd never cared about me and sex between us was just a habit, it didn't mean anything so we argued all day and he said he'd never forgive me for ruining his birthday. Oh well, I would never forgive him for making my family stay at a hotel in town and not in our house in April when they'd come down for my birthday. Charmaine started on me saying that I'd ruined her Daddy's birthday and that I'm not good enough because I don't spend money on her like her Nan does, and how poor Nanny has to save to buy her a computer when I had the money to buy her one but didn't. So here are two people in the home saying that they don't care about me. The only way out of this hurt is to become hard like Wayne and not care, then no one can ever hurt me again.

Saturday 20th June

Wayne sort of made it up to me then started fighting with me again so I lay in bed as much as I could to stay away from him. He wouldn't leave me alone so I screamed that I was going to pack and Wayne screamed back that he loved me and didn't want me to leave so we got along better after that for the sake of peace in the house. We just seem to be going over the same ground and I'm starting to get really frustrated and wanting something done about this constant fighting, making up, fighting and making up. #

Sunday 5th July

I was really sick after breakfast, couldn't stop vomiting so I lay down because I couldn't keep my head up. Every time I got up I vomited and couldn't even keep water down so I had Wayne take me to town at 5pm. Pam had to meet us at the edge of town and take me to the hospital because Wayne was drunk and shouldn't have been driving. I had three blood tests and stayed for hours for observation because I was dehydrated. Wayne drove home while we stayed at Pam's and the kids and I didn't sleep because it was so noisy there.

Monday 6th July

Wayne dropped in to Pam's after work. I hadn't eaten since Saturday lunch and was still really weak. Despite my state, he argued with me about him having to do all of the work and when

I responded in defence of my sickness he said: 'If you have the energy to fight with me then you can get off your fucking arse.' The ferocious way he said it made me yell at him saying: 'I wish I was dead just to get away from you,' and he said: 'You're always sick, why don't you just die,' so I called him a pig. He went outside and Pam ran out after him to commiserate on how awful I was to her darling boy. The way Wayne gets on with her is abnormal, they sit in her kitchen talking like lovers, giggling all the time whenever we have to stay in town and all I get are grunts from him. I feel so alone.

Friday 10th July

As if I couldn't feel any more alone Charmaine told me I talk garbage and to stop talking to Wayne about her Nan behind her back. She doesn't care that hers and my relationship has deteriorated to the point of no return because Pam continually tells her that I am a rotten mother and that Charmaine can live with her.

Thursday 1st October

Wayne snarled at me this morning so I called him a pig and he said: 'Takes a cunt to know one.' I didn't talk to him for the rest of the day. I was so sick from this cold that I can't shake, I slept in the afternoon.

Thursday 8th October

Lately I have to contend with Pam almost as much as with Wayne. I went downtown and bought Charmaine and Louise shorts so Pam went straight downtown after I gave the girls the shorts and outdid me, buying them half a wardrobe of clothes plus toys. I later took Louise to the doctor for her constipation which was so bad the kid had stomach cramps and he said that she had to change her diet. I told Pam because she was the one feeding them junk food by the truckload and she yelled at me for daring to criticise her parenting. Then she turned on Wayne and me, saying: 'Is it pick-on-me time?' then to Wayne: 'You don't believe in that trash the doctor told Debbie, do you?' Then she said: 'Damian and Deidre wouldn't deprive their kids of an ice block and I'm not going to. They can't miss out on things, the poor kids.' (My children were having huge packets of chips, bags of lollies, flavoured milk and soft drinks, as much of whatever they wanted every time Pam babysat them.) *The 'discussion' turned into a screaming match resulting in Pam saying I was a crazy hippie and not talking to me for the next week.*

During that week of ignoring me she was overly friendly with the kids and Wayne, repeatedly telling him that he should divorce me and let her take over the kids fulltime. Following these conversations with his mother, Wayne often taunted me saying that I should leave and let the kids have a mother they loved. His words struck fear and despair in me and became a form of abuse far more hurtful than the physical hurt he inflicted.

Thursday 15th October

Barry (Wayne's father) turned out to be an unexpected ally today. He came out to the property, and while he was here Charmaine abused me saying that she hated me because I didn't do anything for her, not like Nan did. Barry told Wayne that he'd have to do something about Charmaine as she was becoming uncontrollable. Then he said to Charmaine: 'That's rubbish that your Mum does nothing for you. She does everything for you and you should respect her.' Charmaine didn't talk to me for days after this and continued to worship Pam, taunting me with threats of living in town with her Nanny who loved her. She told me that Wayne and Pam didn't want me to be her mother anymore.

Wednesday 25th November

Charmaine yells at me almost every day and I am a nervous wreck. Wayne kicks up a stink whenever I want to go somewhere that he doesn't. (I only ever went downtown to shop for something we needed. Until Charmaine played regional basketball, the entire time I was with Wayne I went to the movies twice, with the girls, never out to dinner or even a coffee unless my family was visiting and only to functions involving his family.) *He won't let me drive the car unless he's with me and has begun to take the keys to the other car with him, locking the front gate when he goes to work so (as mentioned earlier) that we are prisoners here. # He treats me like a child who needs constant disciplining regardless of my not needing it.*

Sunday 13th December

For once my injuries weren't due to intentional violence on his part. Tonight, Wayne and I were looking at the brake lights on the car to see whether they worked and he went to hug me. I hated him touching me especially when he was drunk. He staggered to me and we clashed heads. His head split my lip and it bled. I must have had my mouth open as we connected because my tooth connected with the scar on his nose, opening it so that it bled. He thought the incident was funny.

By the end of this year I was resigned to Wayne's violence. I thought I knew what he was capable of and that he'd done his worst to me. Believing that I had seen that and survived gave me the misguided confidence that I could handle any future abuse. I couldn't foresee violence worse than what I'd experienced in the past and so within our relationship my manner was less subservient. As I became less malleable he showed more indifference toward me, oddly enough. The abuse became less physical and frequent: I wasn't even worth slapping. It was as if I'd been a work in progress and now no longer suited his needs, although we continued with sex as usual. Wayne's physical abuse may have lessened, however his indifference translated itself into a stronger alliance with his mother. I began to have serious concerns that their conspiring to take Charmaine from my care would result in my first-born child living with her Nan in town permanently. After all, I was the only one in this group opposed to the idea. Charmaine hated me by now and would have loved to be with Pam, such was hers and Wayne's influence. The fear of losing my children one by one to this domineering woman had been the key to my staying with Wayne as long as I did. Yet the longer Pam continued to have the dominant role in the girls' upbringing, the more fear turned to concern for the girls' mental stability.

This concern prompted my decision to leave, as much as it was Wayne's abuse towards me.

1999

Friday 1st January

Why not start this year the same as any other by Wayne fighting with me? He gets so picky and nasty when he drinks and today was no exception. After his arguing with me he went up to the bedroom depressed, which was a new development. Normally after a fight he would snap back to normal, forget he'd fought and expect me to do the same. #

Saturday 2nd January

I am drinking wine daily when I'm at home. I don't drink enough to stop me from caring for my kids but it takes the edge off the unbearable pain I feel every day. The wine gives me a measure of joy. When I drink, I can pretend Charmaine loves me. I love being at home with Kirra who is the happiest child. She plays in the garden for hours while I landscape with rocks we find on the property, then we dance to records in the afternoon. Louise continues to have chest infections and middle ear infections and Charmaine has been vomiting most of this week, no doubt due to the disgusting diet Pam feeds them. Thank goodness, I have Kirra out here most of the time and funnily enough she is the only one who doesn't get sick constantly.

Deborah Thomson

Wednesday 13th January

Mum and Grandma are here to celebrate Christmas just gone. Wayne actually let them stay in the house # and I am so happy to see them it's unbelievable. While Wayne was at work we had a cheese and fruit platter on the front verandah and I felt so relaxed and normal. Charmaine was uptight and rude to everyone so Mum took her up to her bedroom and talked to her. Later she came down from the bedroom and told me that Charmaine thinks I hate her because I treat her differently to Nan. (Pam had taught the girls that being overly indulged equated to being loved and because I didn't indulge Charmaine in that manner, the poor kid was confused and thought I hated her.) Mum said that I need to show Charmaine that I love her. She is very insecure around me because I am so different toward her in comparison to Pam. Wayne's mother has so much to account for with her obsessive behaviour. She's destroyed Wayne and is fast ruining Charmaine.

Thursday 14th January

Grandma and Mum are leaving tomorrow so I stayed up with them tonight for as long as possible to try and drag out their time here. The two days have flown and I didn't want to go to bed because they'll be gone soon. I'm already feeling sick from knowing that the only family I have won't be back for at least a year.

Friday 15th January

We had to drop Mum and Grandma at the Bus Terminal ages before their bus left and I couldn't wait with them because Wayne was in a hurry and didn't want to wait, even though all we did after dumping (that's what it felt like) my family off was to go to Pam's so that she could spoil the girls rotten and tell them how weird my family was and that their leaving was 'good riddance to bad rubbish'.

Friday 5th February

I had an argument with Pam over her buying a dress for Charmaine for her school dance when she knew I'd been wanting to buy it. I'd love to have had the opportunity to dress my own children but Pam always got in first. She wouldn't listen to me when I begged her to let me buy clothes for the girls and yelled at me saying that she wanted to bring them up her own way, including how they were clothed and that I didn't matter because I was a crappy mother. I'd never had the chance to be a mother to Charmaine or Louise so how would Pam know what sort of mother I was?

Just how much control Pam and Wayne had over the girls, in particular the eldest, from the very beginning is indicated by the following. Charmaine was 18 months old when she suddenly began to cry hysterically each time she was at Pam's and she realised that I was leaving the house to go to work. She would not be consoled, grasping at my legs and crying pathetically as though her heart was breaking: 'Don't go Mummy, don't leave me.' I couldn't bear it and would hesitate, picking her up and hugging her while looking to Wayne to let me stay a little longer until Charmaine had calmed down. We were self-employed and starting shifts half an hour later would not have mattered. Both Pam and Wayne weren't having what they saw as my interference with the status quo so Charmaine would be dragged from my arms by Pam and simultaneously I'd be pulled out the front

Deborah Thomson

door to the car by Wayne. As far as they were concerned I had no authority over the situation and Charmaine's crying for me was of little consequence. After two weeks of similar behaviour from Pam and Wayne in response to Charmaine's hysterical behaviour, she finally gave up expecting me to console her and from that point on she looked to Pam for love and comfort.

Saturday 6th February

Pam called us at home to say she couldn't find the keys to one of our contract cleaning jobs. She had this horrible hysterical tone of voice and was so stressed about the keys that I became stressed. Wayne of course turned on me and blamed me saying that I'd been the last one to see the keys. While he and I were arguing, Pam said that she'd just found the keys but it was too late. Wayne had by now screamed at me I was 'a stupid cunt for losing the keys'. Pam hung up with a self-satisfied goodbye as if she knew that her stressing had the effect of making Wayne blame me for whatever was upsetting her. Like a trained monkey, he does blame me and she gets immense satisfaction from that.

Tuesday 9th February

Pam had been at Wayne all week putting me down and saying that he should get rid of me, to the extent that he was stressed and so angry he snapped at me all the way through work. As I was getting into the car at the end of work he purposely kicked me as he sat in the driver's seat, in the corner of my eye and it bled from a cut. The kick really hurt and I cried the entire way home. He said it was an accident but I couldn't be bothered listening to his ridiculous, pathetic excuses.

Wednesday 10th February

His parents saw the cut on my eye and believed Wayne when he said it was an accident. Not that Pam would care if she knew the truth. Her 'darling boy' can do no wrong.

Thursday 11th February

Pam left her Serapax tablets (a strong sedative for anxiety) *in her open handbag hanging on the kitchen door and Kirra got into them. She had one to her lips when we got back from work! Pam said that it wasn't her fault. (She'd done the same thing when Wayne was two years of age and he'd had his stomach pumped. Wayne dropped me at the outpatients with Kirra because we had no idea how many tablets she'd taken and I was there for three hours. Kirra didn't need her stomach pumped, thank God. Pam takes the strongest dose she's allowed and she always leaves her bedroom door open where there are tons of pills and the kids can just walk in and help themselves. Wayne continues to let Pam look after the girls even though she's doped up and not even with it half the time. I'm going crazy trying to make any changes to the babysitting arrangement. Anyway, it's probably too late to change it now that Charmaine and Louise are so dependent on her to buy them things.*

Saturday 27th February

Pam took the girls shopping and came home crying saying that they were uncontrollable animals. Charmaine was the rudest she's ever been today, even to Pam who turned around and said that it was my fault, I needed to be firmer with Charmaine! I was incredulous when she said that, as I've told her for years that she's been spoiling Charmaine and that this might have bad repercussions. At least Pam doesn't have Charmaine telling her that she hates her every half an hour, the way the child does to me.

Monday 12th July

Wayne screamed at me so much at Kentish House (a cleaning contract we had) *yesterday that I couldn't talk to him today. I've never hated him as much as I do right now and I don't think I'll ever get over this hate. Charmaine, Wayne and Pam hate me so I might as well feel the same to them in return.*

Sunday 5th September

Pam is smothering the girls and showering them with presents, really expensive ones so much so that they all want to live in town with her. I can't lose my children to Pam. There is nothing else in this stinking life that I have to cherish if I lose them.

The year consisted of Pam dominating me and virtually taking over the rearing of the girls. I was back at work most weekdays as Pam seemed to injure herself regularly, telling us she was unable to work for us in the business but could babysit in exchange. There was a marked reduction of violence in the home. Wayne had little time to abuse me because we'd bought a merry-go-round/chair-o-plane and spent every other weekend taking that to fetes and functions. When we weren't out with the merry-go-round we drove Charmaine to basketball matches around the state where she competed in the regional basketball competition. For the first time since our marriage, due to Charmaine's selection in the Alka Springs basketball team and the merry-go-round commitments, Wayne was taking us places. Being in the public eye to such a degree meant that he could not hit me or scream at me as often as he had in the past.

2000

Friday 21st January

Huge fight tonight with Wayne throwing things everywhere in the lounge room and at me in front of the kids, screaming his lungs out the whole time (and Pam blames me for the kids being uncontrollable). Then he picked up the lounge at one end and tried to throw it across the room and yelled at me to get out. He screamed that I'd never see the kids again and he'd shoot me if I came near them. Of course, he later said that he wanted me to stay and the usual stuff: 'You're my world, I can't live without you …' I stay because I won't go anywhere without the kids even though I could do without the abuse Charmaine gives me three quarters of the time.

Sunday 30th January

Pam called me an irresponsible bitch to Wayne, something else he can add to his vocabulary when he's screaming at me.

Friday 18th February

Wayne and I had a huge screaming fight. All the resentment I've felt over the years of rotten treatment is emerging so much that I feel sick and physically shake when we're fighting. I don't like him sometimes; he knows it and gets cranky and moody for days at a time. I've been trying to escape into the bedroom when he's at home or out in the garden but whenever I'm alone for more than half an hour he comes looking for me as if he can't be alone with his own thoughts. # He acts as if he doesn't like me when he does find me yet there's this strange compulsion that he has to know where I am and what I am doing when I'm not with him. # It is wearing and tiring and by the time he goes to work I am utterly exhausted from his presence, because I'm constantly waiting for his mood to change and for him to scream at me. #

Sunday 20th February

No matter what is happening during the day, Wayne still demands sex. I can't go to bed at 6.30pm like he does so I have to wake him up when I go to bed on his orders to do my duty. Knowing that I can't avoid him I hate the nights. There's no peace for me even when he goes to bed early.

Tuesday 22nd February

Wayne said that he didn't love me anymore. The way he said anymore was different to the other times he'd said something similar. It gave me a shock because I'd always told myself that he wouldn't kill me if he thought he loved me. Now I wondered what would prevent him from doing that if he got angry enough.

Sunday 27th February

After work Wayne confided in me following a particularly vicious argument between him and his mother when we picked up the kids. He told me that his Mum had always blamed his drinking and drug taking as a teenager for her taking Serapax. He said that she had always loved Damian more and that she'd made his life hell with her constant nagging and stressing and fighting. She is the most down and negative person I've ever met and I can only imagine the horrible upbringing Wayne had received from her. I hate going to her house every day and having to put up with her stress. The stress is palpable even though she's not talking to me at the moment.

Monday 28th February

After what Wayne said yesterday I wondered if he'd started going out with me thinking that I'd save him from his mother's influence. If that is true, I don't want the responsibility of saving him. I feel sorry for him. However, I feel like he's sucking me dry with his nonstop talking or yelling at me when he's here at home and I'm getting more and more depressed. At least he's not fighting with me at the moment.

Tuesday 29th February

I'm buoyed by the lack of fighting. Wayne said he did love me and that he'd said that he didn't the other night in the heat of the fight. I don't believe him. He did mean it but maybe we can turn a corner if he continues to treat me like a human being.

The entry above is evidence of the cycle of violence in action: his pursuing me, following that, the honeymoon phase then by the following morning the build-up and stand-over phase, followed by the inevitable explosion. It was always the same over a matter of days.

Deborah Thomson

Sunday 5th March

The truce didn't last for long. Wayne fought with me this morning. He was really angry and got the gun out to shut me up and screamed that he was taking the kids and that I wouldn't have a chance to get them back because he and his mother would make sure he kept them. I had to get down on the floor and keep quiet so that he'd calm down. I lay there for a while. He took his wedding ring off and smashed it flat so I took mine off later and ripped up some wedding photos because I was so upset at being made to lie down in front of him earlier like a whipped dog, just to stop him shooting me. He fought with me until he went to sleep and he told me that my queer family was never staying here again.

Monday 6th March

Wayne rang from town to see if I was still at home and hadn't left. As he had done in the past, he said that he'd try to be a little better then he straightaway said that I should stop being so cranky, as if it's me alone who causes these fights. # As soon as he said that I knew he wouldn't change his ways.

Saturday 18th March

We lost Kirra downtown for half an hour and we had to go to the police station to report her missing. A woman who knew our family found her and gave her to Charmaine who'd gone off looking for Kirra while we were at the station. She'd walked to the bus terminal park to play like she had once before for her cousin Allan's birthday. She had somehow remembered the location of the park. Immediately we had her back with us Wayne screamed at me as if I was the only one at fault for losing Kirra.

Whenever there's a crisis he and Pam scream blame at me, they never apologise regardless of whose fault it is. I'm fast disappearing into a black hole and sometimes I don't even think I exist except to be screamed at whenever Wayne and Pam are stressed.

Thursday 6th April

Had to do the shopping, then went to work, then put the blood pressure monitor on my arm I'd been given to wear. The blood pressure measurement went up to 186/110 while I was at Pam's place. I knew being there made me uptight but that was ridiculous.

Thursday 13th April

Mum and Grandma came down for three days to have an early birthday celebration for me and true to his word Wayne wouldn't let them stay in our house, they had to stay in a flea-bitten hotel in town and pay for the accommodation themselves. Their room was upstairs with so many stairs to climb that Grandma's heart hurt, which worried me as she'd had heart attacks recently.

This visit was the last time she'd come to Alka Springs. She died in October that year from multiple heart attacks.

Friday 14th April

Wayne dumped Mum and Grandma at the Bus Terminal as always and we left. He wouldn't wait for the bus to arrive. Mum rang us later while we were having a break at Pam's to say that their bus was leaving later in the evening so after we finished the afternoon work we picked them up from the terminal (they'd been there all day sitting on plastic benches). Wayne left their bags at the service station next door and took them to Vinnies where they had to wait until we'd finished the cleaning. Pam arrived and dropped the girls off then Wayne went back to Pam's while we walked to Tatts for dinner. We were only there for 45 minutes when Wayne came back and dropped Mum and Grandma back at the terminal. Again, we didn't wait as Wayne was hurrying to get home. Charmaine had ignored Mum and Grandma through dinner and didn't say goodbye either. (Pam had so often told Charmaine that my family was weird and disgusting that she'd completely alienated the child from my side of the family, in order for Charmaine to love only her and Wayne.) *It was the last time I saw my grandmother alive.*

Saturday 6th May

Wayne screamed at Kirra for nothing so I screamed at him to leave her alone. He was acting like a maniac throwing himself around the lounge room screaming so I told him to stop acting crazy and he called me a bitch and a whore then went to bed.

Friday 8th June

A huge fight tonight, Wayne was so angry he ordered me to leave and said I could take Kirra but Charmaine and Louise were staying with him. The kids were crying and didn't want me to leave with Kirra and split them from their sister. I wouldn't go without all three of them so tried to stay calm in the midst of Wayne's screaming in the hope that he'd calm down quicker.

His repeated threat that I'd lose the girls if I tried to leave him kept me under his control and diminished (or so I thought) my ability to escape. These factors (his control and my diminished ability to leave) coloured my response to his continual abuse in that I shifted responsibility for his abusive behaviour onto myself. This was easy to do since he'd either denied the abuse or blamed me for his 'anger' from the beginning of our relationship. His control over my thought processes was such that I minimised the seriousness of the violence and became almost immune to and accepting of his abuse. In doing this, I became his possession.

Subconsciously I knew that Wayne was psychotic, that his explosive temper and unpredictability were more than just 'issues with anger and poor impulse control' (though they were part of the problem). Yet, I gave up my own life to be someone else to the point of feeling grateful to him when he would threaten to kill me and not follow through with those threats—a personality to suit living with an abuser. In essence, it was psychological and physical slavery, virtual captivity.

The repeated trauma eroded my personality and coping mechanisms. Wayne was so controlling and persuasive he had me believing that his anger was my fault. Often, he appeared so rational when telling me that I was at fault for everything negative in our relationship, I would believe that I was the irrational one for upsetting the harmony when I'd confront him with his abuse. This was behavioural conditioning: he defined my role in the partnership in every aspect. He intimidated me, smashed my treasured possessions and constantly told me how ugly, inarticulate, useless and dependent upon him I needed to be. I was physically locked up and isolated from society, controlled to the extent that I had to be with him constantly or he'd have me followed and spied upon. I did what I was told to do, he controlled who I saw, where I went. He limited outside involvement with others while at the same time justifying his actions and twisting my arguments to his benefit. I was there solely to please him—my every waking moment, in his mind, to be employed as a devotion to the fulfilment of his needs. Any deviation to this devotion would incur his anger and hatred. He would mess with my head so that I would be the one feeling guilty, stupid, ugly, demeaned and over-emotional after an abusive episode. It was much later that I came to realise that his chronic abuse was causing serious psychological harm.

Wednesday 28th June

I'm happy at home with Kirra who loves being out in the bush. Then Wayne comes home at night and is so uptight he blames me for the slightest thing then screams when he thinks I'm answering back. He says it is entirely my fault for his anger so that he doesn't have to change. #

Thursday 29th June

I wouldn't wear stockings tonight during sex as I usually had to. I hate being forced to every time so for once wouldn't bow down to his demands. He became angry and locked the bedroom door so that I had to sleep on the lounge which suited me. Wayne has always hated me saying what I think. When I first met his mother she, like Wayne, thought I was quiet and weak, that's why she talked Wayne into staying with me.

Monday 10th July

I weigh 46 kilos and can't put weight on because I'm stressed from being surrounded by extremely stressful people.

Saturday 30th September

Wayne screamed at me as if it was my fault the kids stayed at Pam's last night and he'd had to change his work schedule to bring them home. While he was screaming, he had such an evil look on his face with his eyes completely expressionless that I hid in the bedroom. While we were fighting, Kirra hit Louise on the head with a rolling pin because Louise took her play dough from her. Kirra had hit Louise so hard in the forehead that a huge lump came up immediately. Louise was crying hysterically and later Wayne took a quick look at her and said: 'She'll be right,' and refused to drive her to town to be checked over. He abused me for not keeping an eye on the kids (which I hadn't done because he was screaming at me at the time of the incident).

Monday 9th October

Mum rang to say Grandma had had a heart attack and had been rushed to hospital. She was so concerned about Grandma's health that she offered to pay for me to fly to the Gold Coast so that I could see Grandma but Wayne refused to let me go.

Friday 20th October

Mum rang at 8.30am and said Gran had had another massive heart attack at 3am. They had to resuscitate her and she was now unconscious and may have to go on a respirator. She is really sick, Mum said, and has brain damage. She said that I had to come up straightaway but again Wayne wouldn't let me fly saying it was too expensive so I had to catch a bus and Grandma passed away before I reached her.

Deborah Thomson

Saturday 9th December

Wayne fought with me at work over something his mother had said to him earlier and he threw the mop at me at close range. The handle hit my head and bruised it. A lump came up as well so I left the building but came back soon after as I was afraid I'd lose the kids if I left him.

Wednesday 13th December

Wayne fought with me all morning at home. I scratched both his arms badly when he tried to throw me on the ground to choke me so he kicked me instead and went to get the gun. I ran outside and hid for an hour while he came out screaming for me. When I came inside he'd calmed down and wanted sex so I did to keep him from harming me. We'll somehow have to sort this mess of a relationship out because I absolutely can't leave the kids here with Pam looking after them. She'd ruin them like she has Wayne.

Tuesday 26th December

We'd finally driven to the Gold Coast to spend Christmas with Mum. Wayne got so drunk today that he insulted everyone who'd come for Christmas: uncle Phil, his partner Helen, aunty Pauline, my brother Rick, his partner Helga and Mum so that everyone left early. We started packing the car to go back home tomorrow when Wayne became really belligerent, demanding that I unpack everything in the car to find his favourite t-shirt. He kept piling things back into the car as I was taking suitcases out just to annoy me then he kept butting me with his chest saying: 'Go on, just try and get past me to your Mummy.' I was so frustrated and sickened by his behaviour and the fact that he'd ruined the one family gathering we'd had since Grandma's death, I snapped and punched him hard near the left ear. I then burst into tears and ran inside petrified that my defending myself would make him kill me. Mum locked the door and I lay on the lounge shaking and sick to my stomach from the adrenalin coursing through me. I couldn't believe he'd driven me to violence that wasn't entirely in self-defence and I hated myself for it. He took off in the car and stayed away all night then told me the following day, that he'd spent the night with 'some bird' he'd picked up at the pub.

Saturday 30th December

Since the incident at Mum's, Wayne has been acting as if he's got nothing to lose, that my punching him has given him the licence to act how he wants toward me. (Not that he'd shown restraint until this point.) *Tonight, while we were having sex he kept saying: 'Work with me,' then: 'You're not working with me,' in such a creepy, psychotic voice that he scared me. It made me realise that I was seeing a side to him that he'd toned down previously. My punch had lifted the barrier to his restraint sexually and it felt that what he'd done to me before was nothing in comparison to what he was capable of doing now.*

Dynamics were changing between Wayne and me. We were both beginning to act as if we had already broken up. Yet, the relationship limped along from habit rather than from necessity. I remember feeling the business, the two houses we now owned and the security that having those gave me, were becoming superfluous. The girls were what mattered. Their emotional wellbeing was now paramount and, because my sanity was shattering, I knew that I would be incapable of caring for them properly the longer I kept up this charade of a marriage. Still, hope can be a cruel master and I occasionally reverted to the belief that Wayne might yet take responsibility for his anger. Living as I did and it being all I knew, I tried to work with what I had. I was still afraid to take that final step into an unknown where it could mean even less control than I had now. At the same time, I told myself if I had no control over my life as it was, then leaving couldn't make things worse, could it?

2001

Wayne found this year's diary and that of 2002. I have to work with memories so the dates and months where events occurred are not exact. Certain memories are seared into the brain, like moving pictures in the pre-conscious, which makes them easily retrievable. Although the time of the year they occurred may be approximate, the memories themselves are infallible.

March

I graduated from TAFE as an Early Childhood teacher and began to work casually at various preschools in Alka Springs. This was the first time I'd worked away from Wayne and outside of our business since 1986. Yet, I wasn't allowed to have my own car so I had to rely on Wayne to drive me to and from work, a task he bitterly complained about doing. # Although driving me somewhere other than downtown to shop and pay bills was an irksome burden he did it because it meant he was still in control, knowing exactly where I was at any given time just as it had always been. # I had never been given keys to our house either, and not having my own keys later proved to be very problematic.

Deborah Thomson

April

Wayne was arguing with me over his mother and her domination of the children (which he said was in my head). I went to our bedroom to leave him alone and as I was shutting the door he barged in and shoved me. He kept shoving me with his chest saying: 'Who's going to stop me? You?' Each time he shoved me I'd almost fall. The wooden floor was hard and from previous experience of falling on it, I didn't want to do so again. The girls were screaming outside the door but Wayne didn't care, he was so furious that nothing was going to stop him from hurting me. He pushed me onto the bed and threw himself on top of me placing his chest over my face and grinding down so that I couldn't breathe. I panicked and tried hitting his back to move him, nothing was making a difference and he just pushed harder into my face. I felt as if I was slowly being smothered and this frightened me almost to the point of insanity. Kirra came running into the room screaming: 'What are you doing to Mummy?' Wayne got up and laughed saying that we were just playing and he left the room. I sat on the edge of the bed in shock not able to think or feel. Kirra put her arms around me and said: 'You have to get out of here, Mummy,' over and over.

Of the three girls, she was the only one to tell me that I couldn't stay any longer. She alone understood the enormity and gravity of the circumstances. I, being the direct recipient of the violence, was a subjective observer. Kirra despite being the youngest was the most objective in the family. She had seen violence in the house for a shorter period than the elder girls therefore her immunity to the chaos was less ingrained and she could appraise the situation more accurately. She could clearly see that I had to leave because things weren't going to improve. I felt that she saw Wayne for what he truly was: a man out of control who believed that violence was his only option. I still marvel at her maturity at this time. She was only four years old but could see clearly that the family was disintegrating and my life was in danger. Of course, she did not put it in these words but the anguish that prompted her words 'You have to get out of here, Mummy,' was the first time any of the children had expressed a real concern for my long-term safety. The succinctness of her words struck a chord and they drove home a message that I needed to hear.

August

If my memory serves me, Barry died of a heart attack during this month. It fell to me to identify his body at the hospital as no one else in the family would do it. Barry may not have sided with me through everything that happened; however, he was the person I knew who was the closest to an ally. His death left a hole and contributed to an increased apprehension regarding where my life with Wayne was heading. I had a strong sense that there was now nobody in this family who would support me in a crisis.

October

Wayne was yelling at me while I was hurriedly cooking his lunch so that he'd have time to eat it before he had to leave for work. I was wondering why he was so angry over, what seemed to me, nothing to be annoyed about. Suddenly he was in front of me while I had the fridge door open getting things out for the meal. He slammed the fridge door jamming my hand and making me drop the plate of food I was holding at the time. My hand really hurt and I cried out in fright and surprise. His response was to lean harder into the door, sneering at me to pull my hand free. He walked back to the dining room table and continued yelling at me, so I picked up the plate and threw it in the direction of his voice. It was purely a fluke that the plate hit him in the side of his head while the force of my throw had drawn blood from a substantial wound. I was shocked to realise I'd been driven to such a temper that I'd given him a bleeding head wound, and ran out of the room disgusted with myself. I had never intended for the plate to hit him when I'd thrown it, the action was simply a result of frustration and despair. Funnily enough, after the accident he acted as if he was proud of me for resorting to the same level of violence he'd often used during confrontations.

December

Wayne and I went to town for work while Kirra was in the back seat of the car. As we reached the top of the Point (halfway to town from our property), Wayne began arguing about what was a typical argument between us, that of his mother's dominance over the three girls' lives. I responded in a way that only incensed him further and drove him to yell louder. Suddenly he unclipped my seat belt and opened my car door in one swift movement then began pushing me out of the moving car. The car was moving at a fast pace and I was terrified that I'd be pushed onto the bitumen and sustain severe injuries. I managed to pull myself upright and fend him off but this did not stop him from pushing me, trying still to get me out of the car while attempting to drive it. I broke down and begged him to stop, apologising profusely for denigrating his wonderful mother. He pulled over to the side of the road and said that he accepted my apology. How very magnanimous of him! He was not concerned about his action's effect on Kirra who, by now, was crying loudly.

2002

June

It was a Monday around the beginning of June. I was at home with Wayne and the girls at around 2pm. We started arguing about his mother and her influence over Charmaine. I was standing at the kitchen door when he screamed: 'Piss off.' I turned to leave and Wayne was in the kitchen about two feet from me. He took a run-up and kicked me twice in the right buttock cheek with his steel capped work boots, so hard that I lifted off the ground and was thrust forward. The pain was indescribable and later I developed jet black bruises over a large portion of my cheek. Louise and Kirra were standing on the hallway steps in direct eyesight of him kicking me. They clung to each other and yelled: 'Don't hurt Mummy.' The look on their faces of fear and horror from what they'd just witnessed propelled the decision to leave.

I knew I had to go so I grabbed my handbag and walked to the bottom of the property. Normally if I walked out of the house I would wait awhile and return, instead I kept walking along the main road to the church on the junction five kilometres away. I sat beside the church for a couple of hours thinking that I couldn't live like this anymore. I thought about going back home but the looks on the kids' faces made me get up and keep walking towards the nearest town, Urindy. I walked a further two kilometres when it started to rain. It was freezing and becoming dark and I was so cold, without a coat to wear. A young farmer with pups in his car pulled up and offered me a lift to Urindy. It was too late to turn around and he didn't look dangerous so I accepted the lift and he dropped me on the main street by a phone box. (I remember thinking at the time, that getting into a car with a stranger, at nightfall was far less dangerous than returning home to Wayne's violence.) I rang my aunt Pauline, telling her a little about my situation and she urged me to ring the nearest women's shelter. I looked in the telephone book and found the number for the refuge in Alka Springs and called them. It was too late for anyone from there to pick me up so they directed me to the Urindy caravan park where I stayed overnight. The following day a refuge employee took me to Alka Springs and I was housed in a caravan in the Alka Springs caravan park for five days. The refuge coordinator wanted me to press charges but I was too scared of Wayne to do that. Besides, I worried over what would happen to the kids if I charged him but wasn't there with them when the police came to the house.

I was hysterical during the entire time I spent in the caravan. I kept asking for the girls but no one in the refuge took them from our house. An investigation needed to happen before such action could be taken. On Wednesday, two days after I'd left, I rang Wayne as I desperately needed to speak to the children. He refused the first time I called so on the second call I threatened him with legal intervention if he didn't let me talk to the kids. When I spoke to them on the phone, true to my worst fears, they'd been in town with Pam since I had walked out. It seemed to me Charmaine and Louise were excited about her taking them to McDonalds, the movies and clothes shopping, rather than being concerned about my disappearance. I went back to Wayne at the end of the week, regardless of the protests of the refuge staff. I left there to return home because I believed, after years of being told so by Wayne and Pam, that I wouldn't have the children if I left home. They would tell the court that I was insane and an incompetent parent.

July

Wayne and I began attending counselling with an Anglican woman counsellor. We only went twice because on the first occasion she said we were equally at fault and that I should change my behaviours so that Wayne wouldn't be so angry! Of course, Wayne loved hearing this and when we left the building that first time he said: 'See, I told you that it was your fault. I like that counsellor and I'm happy to go back to her.' Within a fortnight of our second visit to her we were fighting exactly as before. I tried to discuss my new-found knowledge given to me from the refuge regarding cycles of violence, anger management strategies and reasons for the occurrence of domestic violence, but Wayne didn't want to listen. # What I was saying was rubbish, he said, so I ended up feeling like I was defending myself in the arguments.

November

Wayne came home drunk at about 7.30pm. I could smell the alcohol on his breath and he had that belligerent demeanour I always associated with him drinking too much. The girls and I continued to watch TV in the lounge room hoping that he'd stop being picky, but he went into the family room where the bar was and kept drinking. He put a record on and played it so loudly the noise drowned out the TV, so we had to go up to Charmaine's bedroom where I tried to read stories to the girls. Wayne kept playing the Radiator's (an Australian rock band) song 'Give Me Head' over and over, singing to it at the top of his voice. Louise went into her bedroom eventually. Charmaine lay on the top bunk in her bedroom while I lay with Kirra in the bottom bunk, wishing there was a lock on the bedroom door. I couldn't sleep because of the noise Wayne was making and the volume he played the music at. It was about 11pm when he started screaming about sluts and wanting sex then playing the song 'Give Me Head' again, making grunting noises, moaning and groaning. I was terrified because I knew from the noise he was making that things were going to escalate. Soon after, he came into Charmaine's room and grabbed my leg dragging me out of the bed. I had my arm around Kirra at the time so she was half-dragged out as well before I fully comprehended what was happening. He dragged me to the bedroom door along the floor by both legs. When we reached the door, he kneed me in the chest twice then grabbed me by the arms and hauled me upright. Then he dragged me to the end of the hallway. He opened the back door and threw me onto the verandah. I banged my right elbow and grazed it. He locked the door screaming that I could stay outside like the dog that I was. I wasn't fit to live inside. I cried to be let in saying: 'Please don't do this,' and he said that, if I wanted to come in, I should walk around the side of the house to our bedroom balcony and come in through that door. I couldn't walk on the rough ground in the dark and barefoot, plus there was a family of red-bellied black snakes living under the bedroom balcony that I didn't want to risk disturbing. So, I stayed where I was. Eventually he let me in, threw me on our bed and said: 'Get into bed if you know what's good for you.' He tried to suffocate me like the last time then rolled over and kneed me in the back so hard I thought my spine had broken. I tried to get on my other side away from him when he got up and locked the door. (Our bedroom was the only one in the house that could be locked.) The kids were now wide awake and banging on our door screaming: 'Leave Mummy alone,' and he screamed: 'I'll fucking do what I want, who's going to stop me?' He started to pace up and down beside the bed saying: 'I'm going to blow, I'm going to do something bad.' I was nearly vomiting from fear then just as suddenly as it all began, he stopped pacing, unlocked the door, played more music downstairs then slept in the lounge room for the night. The following day he acted as if nothing had happened, all was normal and we went to work, nothing said about last night's rage. # The girls must have been as confused as I was but I knew from past experience that questioning Wayne about it would anger him so it was best not to address the elephant in the room.

December / Christmas Day

For once we stayed at home rather than celebrate at Pam's house.

Unfortunately, this gave Wayne licence to drink himself to excess. So, he was again drunk and rampaging through the house ready to unload the stress he'd been building up over the last few days. He usually relied on sex to relieve his tension and today was no exception. He 'requested' sex and when I refused as I was entertaining the girls at the time he began to yell. His yelling quickly turned into threats that he would go to the bedroom and load the rifle then 'blow me away for all the good I was' to him. Charmaine grabbed the cordless phone and attempted to call the police however Wayne wrenched the phone from her and smashed it on the ground. He screamed at her never to side with me again or she'd regret it. Charmaine began to cry and this defused the situation enough for me to take the girls into their bedroom to play with their presents for the remainder of the afternoon. Wayne slept his intoxication off and I gave him what he'd wanted earlier, when the girls had gone to sleep for the night. Another wonderful, memorable Christmas day.

December 31st / New Year's Eve

Kirra took me into mine and Wayne's bedroom after he'd gone to work, saying that she wanted to show me something. She led me to one of the clothes cupboards where there was a gap between it and the wall. There in the gap was one of Wayne's rifles: a short-barrelled ten-shot semi-automatic, one of three guns he'd not handed in during the amnesty following the Martin Bryant shootings in Port Arthur, Tasmania. Kirra told me that Daddy had taken the gun down from the roof in her presence and put it beside the cupboard, back far enough that I probably would not have noticed it, had Kirra not told me. She said he'd told her that he was going to shoot Mummy with it if she was naughty. At first, I couldn't believe he'd stooped so low as to involve a four-year-old in his madness but Kirra showed me a drawing she'd done soon after the incident. It depicted a stick-figure Wayne, with fangs and a rifle shooting a stick-figure me, with blood spurting out. So, I knew that he had done just that and involved her. I suddenly knew that I had to remove the children from him. I spoke to Mum on the phone, disclosing a little about Wayne's violence but that was enough for her to send me pamphlets on 'Domestic Violence and what to do when it was happening to you'. She came down and stayed for two days to give me support. The visit was unsuccessful due to Wayne yelling at her the entire time to mind her business and get out. I had planned to go to the Gold Coast for her 60th birthday party anyway so she and I decided we'd further discuss my leaving the house with the kids when I came up. Leaving was beginning to look like a possibility.

[Above: Kirra's drawing spoken of in the diary entry (New Year's Eve 2002)]

2003

Sunday 5th January

The girls were staying at Pam's overnight leaving Wayne and I alone in the house. At 7.30pm Wayne said goodnight and went to bed. I was in the lounge room eating dinner and watching TV when he appeared in the hallway entrance completely naked. He said: 'Come on up and we'll do it.' I said no. We'd been arguing all day and I didn't want to be close to him in any way. He went back to the bedroom without a word then screamed from the room that I was a slut and a whore. He yelled for the next fifteen minutes that I was a bitch and 'not worth anything'. I was alone with him. Anything could happen and I knew he wouldn't let up so went up to the bedroom and said: 'Fine let's do it.' He said: 'I want it a bit rough. You never get into it and I want you to get into it.' I was surprised and asked him if he enjoyed S & M and he said that he loved 'that sort of thing'. I just sat there feeling sick because I sensed that the sex this time was not something he wanted over and done with quickly, as was normally the case. I said: 'I don't know how to be a prostitute,' (I do not intend any disrespect to sex workers) *and went to leave. He got angry and said: 'I'll show you,' and punched me twice in the face then threw me off the end of the bed. I lay on the ground where I'd landed, dazed, and he jumped off the bed landing on top of me. He straddled my chest so that I was pinned and repeatedly tried to shove his penis in my mouth. He had an erection. I knew then that he was turned on from the violence and I became really scared. My mouth remained closed while he kept trying to put his penis in yelling: 'Suck on this, you bitch.' I wouldn't so he got back on the bed and lay on his back. He said: 'Get on top, NOW.' I did as he said because this scenario was becoming really weird. He'd never before been so openly violent sexually and the fact that he was now showing no restraint made me very frightened. As I sat on top of him I began crying. I just sat there not moving and he grabbed me trying to move me saying: 'Come on, come on.' I couldn't believe that he was laughing at me while I was crying. I was so sickened and upset by what was happening, together with the humiliation I felt when he laughed at my tears, that I slapped him twice on the face. The slaps weren't hard and they excited him. He continued to laugh saying: 'Yeah, yeah, that's what I want.' He raped me. It was over quickly and when he pushed me off him I ran down the stairs sobbing. Wayne yelled from the bedroom: 'Stop crying you bitch or I'll slam you through the wall.' I slept in the lounge room the rest of the night.*

Wednesday 8th January

Wayne and I had another argument, the same argument we'd been having for weeks about me going to my Mum's 60th at the Gold Coast where, according to Wayne, I'd be 'slutting around'. The kids were again staying in town with Pam. Wayne went to bed at 8pm and locked the bedroom door. He screamed through the door: 'You're a slut. You want to go up there and slut around, you're an arsewipe.' He heard me go into Charmaine's room (I intended to sleep in her bed) and this infuriated him even more. He yelled: 'I'm getting the gun now, I'm loading it now and I'm going to shoot your head off with it now.' I was alone with him. I knew the gun was within easy reach and I feared that he really would carry out his threat so I stayed really quiet. He didn't say any more after that and didn't come out of the room. I slept in Charmaine's bed, after barricading the door as best I could and staying awake for the remainder of the night to keep watch.

Thursday 9th January

When Wayne went to work, I rang the refuge in tears over the last two episodes of violence and the woman on the phone said that I had to leave and to take the kids. I told her I couldn't right then because I was out of town, the front gate was locked and I was without a car. She advised me to involve the police but I was still too apprehensive to do that. The refuge lady said that they now had Wayne on record (since the time I had stayed in the caravan park refuge) and were keeping an eye on him for further abuse. They rang DOCS (Department of Child Safety) and arranged an appointment for me to see them in two days' time.

Wednesday 15th January

At about 12 noon we were driving to town with Kirra and Louise in the back seat of the car. We'd been arguing again about me going to Mum's birthday when Wayne punched me in the right arm twice, while driving, then spat in my face. I began to cry and was still crying after we arrived at his mother's. Pam said: 'What's wrong with her now?' Wayne said: 'Nothing, ask her.' They ignored me then and talked to each other until we went to work.

Thursday 16th January

I went to DOCS for an interview under the guise of going downtown to do the food shopping. After I'd told them about Wayne's assault on me in the car with the children witnessing it they said I wasn't allowed to go back home and that if I did they could by law remove the girls from both of us. They told me we were under investigation and had been for some time. I was then taken to the Alka Springs refuge where arrangements were made for Mum and a friend to drive down and collect us (the three girls and me) and to take us interstate to the Gold Coast for our safety. We were told we should go interstate immediately given the seriousness of the abuse Wayne had subjected me to for so long. More significantly, he had easy access to a number of rifles and had repeatedly threatened to kill me with a gun. (The two factors— access to guns and threats of violence involving guns—takes abuse to a higher level according to authorities.) *Two female DOCS employees took me from the refuge to Pam's house where the girls were being babysat while Wayne was at work. They went into the house with me and had to forcibly remove the girls because Pam was yelling: 'You can't do this to my kids,' while hanging onto Charmaine's arm. She was making so much noise she was frightening the girls who began to cry and the ruckus brought the neighbourhood residents out into the street to watch us. We were taken to the refuge where the girls and I were individually interviewed. What was said by each of us evidently satisfied them as they said we had to stay there and wait for Mum to arrive. Eight hours later she and Trish, a friend, arrived in Trish's van. I was in shock by then, Wayne having called repeatedly* (he was somehow in possession of the refuge's phone number) *threatening to find the location of the actual refuge and 'smash every window in the place' to get to his kids. He spoke to Charmaine on the phone saying that after they'd been taken, Pam had fallen to the floor in front of him clutching her heart and saying she was having an attack. Naturally this greatly upset Charmaine who spat at me, thinking that I'd caused her 'precious Nan to die'. I rang Pam's next-door neighbour who went to Pam to check on her health. Lisa reported back to me that she was sitting in the kitchen, drinking coffee and chatting away to Wayne with no sign of having had a heart attack. Her display (if it had happened at all) had been for the sake of drama. Fortunately, I was able to assure Charmaine that nothing was wrong with her Nan. During one call to me, Wayne said: 'What's the matter with you? Why are you doing this to me? I'm not that bad.'* (Wayne's narcissistic self-opinion from the beginning of our relationship had to be justified at all costs. His defensiveness reflected how he saw himself (and still does), disregarding the abuse or denying it ever occurred. He projected his 'anger', never 'abuse' onto me, believing that I was at fault and to blame for any discord and that I alone was wrong for leaving and, in his words, 'breaking up our family'.) *I was called into a room at the refuge to have a conference with the employees and Mum, and I was again strongly urged to leave with her tonight. All I had on me was the girls' hair and tooth brushes and pyjamas from their staying at Pam's the night before, the clothes on their backs, the clothes I was wearing and $200 in my wallet. Because we lived so far out of town they could not take us to the house to collect more belongings, saying* *that was for the police to arrange, so we left Alka Springs that night with next to nothing.*

What happened after leaving is a story in itself.

Afterword

Statistically, 1% of abusers make positive changes toward their thoughts, behaviours and words. This is such a minute proportion of perpetrators compared with the overall number of abusers that it drove home to me the absolute need to make drastic changes to all of our lifestyles. So, during January2003 I removed myself and the children from immediate danger and innocently assumed Wayne's abuse would end or at least have less impact on us. Instead, after we left his manipulation increased. His concerted effort to have us return to him manifested in continuous phone calls, sometimes twenty within a single evening. Also; stalking, threats of violence towards me, to kidnap the children or to commit suicide unless we re-joined him. In fact, anything he could think of to gain my attention and resume his position of control and domination. Wayne's continued abuse prompted me to begin writing a second book, 'Courting Hope?' recounting the years of litigation regarding custody battles in the Family Court. To a lesser degree the years of counselling required to offset the effects of prolonged abuse will form part of the book's narrative.

Briefly upon arrival at the Gold Coast, after our stay in the

Alka Springs refuge, we shuttled between a Brisbane refuge and various rental accommodations until, finally, the property settlement afforded me ownership of a modest townhouse in Kooralbyn, Queensland. I resumed Early Childhood teaching for a period after which I assumed a lengthy position with Australia Post delivering mail, while completing a certificate in counselling and a diploma in case management. The girls appeared to happily blend school commitments with their personal lives, establishing good friendships and enjoying social activities they'd never had the opportunity to experience while we were with Wayne. My youngest child Kirra and I moved to Tasmania in 2010 into a house I'd bought in Queenstown on the West Coast. Kirra moved to Melbourne for tertiary studies and I moved to the Northwest coast of Tasmania to be with my partner of, to date, six years. I was diagnosed with Late Onset Friedreich's Ataxia, a degenerative neurological disease which affects organ functioning and balance. I have reached the stage where I require full-time care. Mum will soon be relocating from the Gold Coast to be near me as we all negotiate our encroaching 'old age'. Regardless of my and the girls' experiences since leaving Wayne, the hardships, financial deprivations and emotionally draining events that occurred on an almost daily basis were, in hindsight, worth it. The three girls and I could begin to explore what it was to have a life without hypervigilance, without the constant reality of Wayne's explosive anger directed at us, without violence and hate being an essential part of our existence. Where at last, for the first time, we had space to discover our uniqueness as human beings and our capacity to love one another. I have also had the opportunity to reunite with my dad and stepmother Rita, aunt Pauline and uncle Phil ('Fred'), sister and brother respectively of my Mum, all of whom have redefined what it is to have relatives you want to spend time with and who love you.

For the amount of time spent living with an abuser, it takes approximately the same amount of time again to mentally recover from the abuse. This observation made by one of many counsellors I have seen since leaving rang true for me. I was with Wayne for seventeen years and it has taken a further fourteen years to truly feel psychologically free of those years of abuse.

I still suffer from moderate PTSD (post-traumatic stress disorder) and I wake screaming from the occasional nightmare where Wayne is attacking me. However, there is a marked difference between who I was during the relationship and directly after leaving and who I am now, without his abuse. There are people close to me who still retain anger over what happened to me and those who harbour hatred toward Wayne. I feel terribly guilty knowing that staying with Wayne for such a long time has caused heartache and anguish for my family and wish that I had confided in them about the abuse long before I left. Not disclosing the violence to loved ones until the demise of our marriage shocked my family a great deal more than if they'd known I was in an abusive relationship long before we separated.

My children too had mental issues that would take the same amount of time to resolve as the time during which they lived with the abuse. Charmaine, having been in the home the longest (thirteen years), took the most time to recover. She is 27 now, a mother herself and a primary school teacher. From talking to her, it seems that she did indeed resolve the majority of her issues by the age of 26. Louise is a social worker and she too has worked through many of her issues. The youngest, Kirra, is studying to be an art curator. Out of the three girls, she, most of all, understands the destruction Wayne's abuse has caused. Because of this she is better equipped to recognise the subtler forms of domestic violence in her relationships with others, should they be present. For that I am grateful.

If every person who is being abused were to quickly recognise that they are indeed experiencing domestic violence (and it should be named as such), then countless future episodes of violence might be avoided. We, as a society, should continue to openly debate domestic violence. It is gratifying to see that such discussion is increasingly present in the public's consciousness. However, tangible support such as the availability of low-rent housing for those with low incomes, refuges and counsellors specifically trained in domestic violence should be more readily available. In Tasmania, there is a 'Safe at Home' program whereby it is the abuser who is removed from the home by the police rather than the abused. I advocate for such a program to be nationally employed as it makes far more sense that the victim, who is usually traumatised and often experiencing financial abuse, remain at the family residence in familiar surroundings and with easier access to everyday resources. My children's and my own experience of mental recovery suggests that the sooner the abused and their children remove themselves from an abusive and extremely poisonous environment (the alternative being that of the Safe at Home program above), the quicker and longer-lasting their recovery from the after-effects will be.

Despite having come so far in my progress towards good mental health, I still on occasion experience acute shame and guilt for remaining with Wayne and leaving myself open to abuse. I am apprehensive that family members and friends may be judgmental after reading my story. I would not blame them. I hope those close to me do not condemn me for putting up with years of assaults to my physical body and psychological wellbeing. Outside condemnation is often directed toward the abused and not focused upon the abuser's actions enough.

The unseen emotional trauma generated from exposure to domestic violence at an early age persists through lifespans and generations. As such, we desperately need from-the-ground-up education about abuse and its effects. A range of comprehensive educational tools aimed at audiences from early childhood through to adulthood would be effective. These would be geared to each age group's developmental stage and devoted to understanding the dynamics of domestic violence. Tools providing information on how to quickly recognise domestic violence, the effects linked to its exposure and the strategies to combat it are essential to alleviate the burden on both individuals and societies. I hope that my story has helped to do that even to a small degree.

The Personal Safety Survey done in 2012 by the ABS (Australian Bureau of Statistics) and the Australian Institute of Criminology found that domestic violence in Australia is overwhelmingly committed by men against women. Over three times as many incidents are caused by males.

Rates of violence since age 15 by current or former partners:

Women	Men
– 1 in 5 had experienced sexual abuse	– 1 in 22 had experienced sexual abuse
– 1 in 6 had experienced sexual or physical abuse	– 1 in 19 had experienced sexual or physical abuse
– 1 in 4 had experienced emotional abuse	– 1 in 7 had experienced emotional abuse
– 1 in 3 had experienced physical abuse	– 1 in 2 had experienced physical abuse, mainly men against men

- In the years 2008-2010, eighty-nine women were killed by current or former partners. This equates to *nearly one per week.*
- 61% of women surveyed had children in their care with 48% of children having seen or heard violence in the home.
- 58% of women had never contacted police.
- 24% had never sought advice or support.
- It takes an average of *five to seven acts of violence* before the abused person leaves the abuser (**www.anrows.org.au** 2012).

I was one of the people included in those averages. If you are reading this and currently experiencing domestic violence in the home, leave before you too become part of these statistics.

Below are phone numbers to speak to someone who can provide clarity, support and information relevant to domestic violence. I wish I'd had such information when I was with

Wayne, early in our relationship rather than in the latter stages of the marriage. Oddly, those very few who were aware of Wayne's propensity to violence largely ignored his abuse towards me, either accepting it as part of life or not recognising the significance of his behaviour. Speaking to a person who understood violence in the family may have assisted me to leave earlier than I did, thus preventing much of the pain and horror my family felt when they became aware that Wayne had abused me throughout the entire seventeen years of our relationship.

I stayed with him for far too long.

The phone contacts below stand as of July 2016:

- 000 if your life is in immediate danger
- National Domestic Violence Hotline 24-hour support: **1800RESPECT (1800737732)**
- Lifeline 24-hour support: **131114**
- Translating Service: **131450**
- Mensline Australia: **1300789978**
- Kids Help Line: **1800551800**
- National Disability Abuse Hotline: **1800880052**
- Relationships Australia support groups: **1300364777**

Bibliography

http://anrows.org.au/sites/default/files/Violence-Against-Women-Key-Statistics.pdf

www.communities.qld.gov.au/resources/childsafety/practice-manual/prac-paper-domestic-violence

www.pro.psychocentral.com/exhausted-woman/2017/03/13-reasons-why-people-abuse

Whose Life Is It Anyway?

Deborah Thomson

			Qty
ISBN: 9780648150862			
	RRP	AU$24.99	.....
Postage within Australia		AU$5.00	.....
		TOTAL* $_____	
		* All prices include GST	

Name: ....

Address: ....

....

Phone: ....

Email: ....

Payment: [ ] Money Order   [ ] Cheque   [ ] MasterCard   [ ] Visa

Cardholder's Name:..

Credit Card Number: ....

Signature:..

Expiry Date: ....

Allow 7 days for delivery.

Payment to: Marzocco Consultancy (ABN 14 067 257 390)
                          PO Box 12544
                          A'Beckett Street, Melbourne, 8006
                          Victoria, Australia
                          admin@brolgapublishing.com.au

Be Published

Publish through a successful publisher.
Brolga Publishing is represented through:
• National book trade distribution, including sales,
marketing & distribution through **Dennis Jones and
Associates Australia.**
• International book trade distribution to
    • The United Kingdom
    • North America
    • Sales representation in South East Asia
• Worldwide e-Book distribution

For details and enquiries, contact:
Brolga Publishing Pty Ltd
markzocchi@brolgapublishing.com.au
PO Box 12544
A'Beckett St VIC 8006

ABN: 46 063 962 443
(Email for a catalogue request)